Targeted Reading

Student Guided Practice Book

comprehension

vocabulary

fluency

phonics

writing

Editors
Conni Medina, M.A.Ed.
Kristy Stark, M.A.Ed.

Assistant Editor
Leslie Huber, M.A.

Editorial Director
Lori Kamola, M.S.Ed.

Editor-in-Chief
Sharon Coan, M.S.Ed.

Editorial Manager
Gisela Lee, M.A.

Creative Director/
Cover Designer
Lee Aucoin

Illustration Manager
Timothy J. Bradley

Designers
Neri Garcia
Lesley Palmer

Photo Editor
Judy Tan

Print Production Manager/
Interior Layout Designer
Don Tran

Print Production
Juan Chavolla
Robin Erickson

Contributing Authors
Christine Dugan, M.S.Ed.
Leslie Huber, M.A.
Margot Kinberg, Ph.D.
Miriam Meyers

Publisher
Rachelle Cracchiolo, M.S.Ed.

Learning Standards: Copyright McREL. www.mcrel.org/standards-benchmarks.

Teacher Created Materials

5301 Oceanus Drive
Huntington Beach, CA 92649
http://www.tcmpub.com
ISBN 978-1-4333-1175-8
© 2009 Teacher Created Materials, Inc. All rights reserved.
Reprinted 2010

Table of Contents

Table of Contents (cont.)

Welcome Letter

Dear Student,

You are starting a reading program that will help you review important skills. Up to this point in school, you have learned many reading strategies and skills. This program will help you focus on what you already know how to do in reading and what you need to learn. You will learn the important reading comprehension strategies and skills and build your fluency and vocabulary.

Sometimes students have trouble learning reading skills. It can seem challenging. This program will help you practice reading strategies and skills every day. Some of these things include previewing text, understanding the problem and solution, and finding the main idea.

Have fun!

Sincerely,

_____

Please sign the bottom of this letter and take it home to share with your parents.

_____

Student Signature

Diagnostic Test

Questions 1–10: Read the passage, look at the map, and answer the questions. Fill in the answer choice you think is correct.

A Southeastern State: Florida

Florida's nickname is the Sunshine State. So it's no surprise that the climate there is warm and sunny. The main reason for its balmy weather? Florida is the southernmost state in the continental United States. Year-round warm weather is why many people come to Florida. About 69 million tourists visit Florida's theme parks, resorts, and beaches each year. Because much of Florida is a peninsula, it has plenty of beaches. Florida's coastline is 1,350 miles long—only Alaska's is longer.

Florida's warm weather especially attracts elderly people. About 30 percent of Floridians are more than 55 years old.

Because Florida is so close to Latin America, it is known as the Gateway of the Americas. Florida draws many immigrants from the Caribbean, especially Haiti and Jamaica. Others come from Central and South American nations, such as Nicaragua and Colombia. About 17 percent of Floridians are Latin Americans.

The island-nation of Cuba is only 100 miles from Florida. Because of its closeness, Cubans make up one-third of Floridians born outside the United States. About one-quarter of the population of Miami is Cuban.

Florida lies at the southeastern edge of the United States.

Growing Fast

Florida is a fast-growing state with a strong economy. The banking business and the computer and electronic equipment industries bring in a lot of money. Another big industry is tourism. A large number of Floridians work in hotels, theme parks, and restaurants.

Like many southern states, the warm climate of Florida is good for growing food. Florida is a center for citrus growing. The state produces four-fifths of all orange and grapefruit products in the United States. It is second only to California in growing vegetables.

Florida's weather isn't always pleasant. The state is in the path of hurricanes. They often strike during summer and fall and cause much damage. Still, Floridians have become used to these storms. For them, the good of living in Florida outweighs the bad.

1 Which sentence tells the main idea of the third paragraph?

- (A) Florida's location is the reason for its warm and sunny climate.
- (B) About 17 percent of Floridians are Latin Americans.
- (C) Florida draws many immigrants from Latin America because of its location.
- (D) Florida has a fast-growing economy.

2 Why is Florida's climate warm and sunny much of the year?

- (A) About 69 million tourists visit Florida's theme parks, resorts, and beaches each year.
- (B) Florida is the southernmost state in the continental United States.
- (C) The state is in the path of hurricanes.
- (D) Florida's coastline is 1,350 miles long.

GO ON

Diagnostic Test *(cont.)*

3 Which question helps you remember information about Florida's climate?

  (A) How many tourists come to Florida each year?

  (B) What crops are grown in Florida?

  (C) Where do most people in Florida live?

  (D) Why is Florida's weather warm and sunny most of the time?

4 The typeface tells you that _____ is an important phrase.

  (A) Growing Fast

  (B) a large number

  (C) warm weather

  (D) these storms

5 This article can help you

  (A) find a hotel in Florida.

  (B) get money for a class trip to Florida.

  (C) learn about Florida.

  (D) get directions to Florida.

6 *A Southeastern State: Florida*

This title tells you that this passage will probably be about

  (A) ocean life.

  (B) every southeast state.

  (C) staying safe.

  (D) Florida.

7 How is Florida like other southern U.S. states?

  (A) It produces four-fifths of all orange and grapefruit products.

  (B) Florida is a fast-growing state.

  (C) It has a warm climate that is good for growing food.

  (D) Cuba is only 100 miles from Florida.

8 What does the caption tell you?

  (A) where Cuba is located

  (B) where Florida is located

  (C) where the United States is located

  (D) why people like to visit Florida

9 Which two bodies of water surround Florida?

  (A) the Atlantic Ocean and the Gulf of Mexico

  (B) Naples and Miami

  (C) the Atlantic Ocean and Cuba

  (D) Haiti and Jamaica

10 If you did not remember how many tourists visit Florida, you could

  (A) read the title.

  (B) read the first paragraph again.

  (C) study the map.

  (D) draw a picture.

GO ON

Diagnostic Test *(cont.)*

Questions 11–18: Read the passage and then answer the questions on the following page. Fill in the answer choice you think is correct.

Eddie Gomez

Dear Jerry,

I'm writing to apologize to you for what happened yesterday. I didn't get a chance to tell you the whole story. So I will now. First of all, I only meant to borrow your bicycle for about 15 minutes. The thing is, I wanted to go to Sound Town to buy a new CD. My mom couldn't take me, and my bike is broken. I was pretty desperate when I saw your bike on your front lawn. I didn't see you around, and the only reason I didn't ring your doorbell was that I didn't want to bother anybody, in case they were sleeping or watching TV or something. Also, I didn't think you'd miss the bike for such a short time. And I guess I thought that somehow if you did notice it was gone, you'd know I took it. I don't know why I thought that.

I guess I should have left a note, but I didn't have any paper handy. Anyway, I was going to bring your bike back as soon as I bought the CD. The problem was, I ran into Jimmy, Angel, and a few of the guys in Sound Town. They wanted to bike over to the mall. I shouldn't have gone with them, but they wanted to get a slice of pizza, and I was hungry.

When the police stopped me at the mall, I was shocked. They said I had stolen your bike. They took the bike and put me in the police car. I told them I only borrowed the bike, but they didn't listen. They just said they were going to arrest me and tell my parents. I was really upset and scared. That's why when they drove me to your house to make sure it was your bike, I freaked out. I yelled at you for calling the police. That was totally wrong. I should have apologized to you right then. Why wouldn't you think someone had stolen your bike? I mean, you had no way of knowing I had borrowed it.

I acted even worse after you and your mom told the police to let me go. I should have thanked you for keeping me out of trouble. But I guess I was too weirded out by what had happened.

Now I realize I was to blame right from the start. I should have asked you first if I could borrow the bike. I had no right to take it (even though I meant to return it—honest). Anyway, I'm really sorry. I hope you will forgive me for the dumb thing I did.

Your friend,
Eddie

GO ON ➡

Diagnostic Test *(cont.)*

11 Which of these is **not** a reason Eddie took Jerry's bike without asking?

Ⓐ Eddie was angry at Jerry.

Ⓑ Eddie's mom couldn't take him.

Ⓒ Eddie's bike was broken.

Ⓓ Eddie didn't want to bother anybody by ringing the doorbell.

12 Because this is a letter, it will probably

Ⓐ have headings and titles.

Ⓑ be written from one person to another.

Ⓒ have study questions at the end.

Ⓓ tell you how to do something.

13 Why did Eddie write this letter?

Ⓐ to apologize for taking Jerry's bike

Ⓑ to ask if he could borrow Jerry's bike

Ⓒ to ask if he could borrow money to go to Sound Town

Ⓓ to ask Jerry where to buy a good bike

14 Which sentence is an opinion?

Ⓐ I didn't have any paper handy.

Ⓑ I ran into Jimmy, Angel, and a few of the guys in Sound Town.

Ⓒ They took the bike and put me in the police car.

Ⓓ I acted even worse after you and your mom told the police to let me go.

15 Eddie was put in the police car **after**

Ⓐ Jerry and his mom told the police to let Eddie go.

Ⓑ he wrote the letter to Jerry.

Ⓒ he took Jerry's bike.

Ⓓ Jerry got his bike back.

16 *Dear Jerry,*

This helps you predict that you will read

Ⓐ an encyclopedia.

Ⓑ a map.

Ⓒ a letter.

Ⓓ a newspaper article.

17 You already know how it feels to make a mistake. This helps you understand

Ⓐ what Sound Town is.

Ⓑ what Jerry's bike looked like.

Ⓒ how to write a letter.

Ⓓ why Eddie wrote an apology letter.

18 *I'm writing to apologize to you for what happened yesterday.*

This topic sentence tells you that Eddie

Ⓐ will ask Jerry for money.

Ⓑ will tell Jerry how to get to Eddie's house.

Ⓒ will tell Jerry that Eddie is sorry for something.

Ⓓ will be invited to a party.

GO ON

Diagnostic Test *(cont.)*

Questions 19–24: Read the passage and then answer the questions on the following page. Fill in the answer choice you think is correct.

The Golden Touch

Once there was a king named Midas who lived in an area that we now call Turkey. Midas was not a bad man, but he was very greedy.

One day a man named Silenus got lost in Midas's kingdom. Midas believed in helping travelers, so he offered to help Silenus return home. Silenus told Midas that he lived with the god Dionysus (dy-u-NY-suhs). Midas arranged to have the man taken home, and soon after, Dionysus appeared before the king.

"I would like to give you a reward for helping my friend," Dionysus said. "Ask me for anything and, if I can, I will grant your wish." Midas knew he had only one wish, so he wanted to be very careful about his choice.

"I would like everything I touch to turn to gold," Midas said. Dionysus looked at the king. "Are you certain that is what you desire?" he asked.

"Yes," Midas answered. "I am positive."

Dionysus granted the king's wish. Midas was excited to immediately put the wish to the test. He touched a twig and a stone—they turned to solid gold. "I got my wish!" exclaimed the king. "Now I will be the richest man in the world!" Midas ran into his palace and touched everything from floor to ceiling. Before he knew it, half the day had gone by and he realized how hungry he was. He went into his dining hall and sat at his golden table.

Midas commanded his servants to bring him food, and they obeyed. Hungrily, Midas grabbed a loaf of bread from the golden plate. As soon as he did, it turned to gold. He took an apple in his hand, but the same thing happened. Midas told his servants to feed him, but as soon as the food touched his lips, it became hard, cold metal. Now he realized his mistake.

"Dionysus!" he cried. "What will I do? I will starve to death because of my wish!"

Dionysus heard Midas and took pity on him. "Not far from your palace is the River Pactolus," he told the king. "Go there and wash yourself in it. Your golden touch will be washed away."

Midas did as he was told, and he was saved. But some of his golden touch remained in the River Pactolus. And to this day, if you look carefully, you can find gold dust there.

Diagnostic Test *(cont.)*

 19 What caused King Midas to fear that he would starve?

Ⓐ His food turned to gold, so he could not eat it.

Ⓑ Dionysus would not give him food.

Ⓒ His servants were angry at him and would not bring him food.

Ⓓ There was no food in the kingdom.

20 Which of these describes King Midas?

Ⓐ jealous and mean

Ⓑ shy and quiet

Ⓒ kind but greedy

Ⓓ friendly but dishonest

21 What was the **first** thing King Midas did after Dionysus granted his wish?

Ⓐ He bathed in the river.

Ⓑ He asked his servants to bring him food.

Ⓒ He asked Dionysus to take away his wish.

Ⓓ He turned a twig and a stone to gold.

22 What problem did the golden touch cause for King Midas?

Ⓐ Everyone became jealous of him.

Ⓑ His food turned to gold, so he could not eat.

Ⓒ Dionysus grew angry at him.

Ⓓ He realized he was bored with gold.

23 Which is a good way to tell someone about King Midas?

Ⓐ King Midas was greedy, so when he got a wish, he wished to change everything to gold. When his wish came true, he found out that the golden touch changed all his food to gold, so he could not eat. He washed himself in the river, and his golden touch went away.

Ⓑ King Midas helped Silenus return home. Then he got a reward. He wanted to change everything to gold, and he did.

Ⓒ King Midas lived in what is now Turkey. He helped a man return home, and then he changed everything to gold. The river still has gold dust in it.

Ⓓ King Midas was a greedy man, so Dionysus gave him a wish. Midas wished to turn everything to gold. Then he asked his servants for food and they brought it to him.

24 People who enjoy reading about _____ would like this story.

Ⓐ famous astronauts

Ⓑ math brain teasers

Ⓒ myths and legends

Ⓓ sports

Name _____

Diagnostic Test *(cont.)*

Questions 25–30: Read the time line and then answer the questions. Fill in the answer choice you think is correct.

Martin Luther King Jr.

Important Dates

1929: Born in Atlanta, Georgia

1948: Became a Baptist minister

1957: Formed the Southern Christian Leadership Conference to fight segregation and gain civil rights for African Americans

1962: Went to jail for protesting segregation in Birmingham, Alabama

1963: Helped organize the March on Washington, D.C. Delivers his "I Have a Dream" speech

1964: Awarded the Nobel Peace Prize

1967: Organized the Poor People's Campaign to get jobs for poor people

1968: Assassinated in Memphis, Tennessee

25 Which one happened **first**?

- Ⓐ Martin Luther King Jr. went to jail for protesting segregation.
- Ⓑ Martin Luther King Jr. was awarded the Nobel Peace Prize.
- Ⓒ Martin Luther King Jr. became a Baptist minister.
- Ⓓ Martin Luther King Jr. was assassinated in Memphis, Tennessee.

26 This passage is about Martin Luther King Jr. You can predict that the time line is about

- Ⓐ settling the American West.
- Ⓑ the American Revolution.
- Ⓒ Martin Luther King Jr.'s life.
- Ⓓ the Civil War.

27 The title tells you that this is about

- Ⓐ the life of Martin Luther King Jr.
- Ⓑ life in the American West.
- Ⓒ how to make something.
- Ⓓ the American Indians.

28 The heading tells you that this is a

- Ⓐ list of new words.
- Ⓑ time line of important dates.
- Ⓒ set of instructions.
- Ⓓ list of names to remember.

GO ON ➡

Diagnostic Test *(cont.)*

29 Which sentence tells you the most important idea?

- Ⓐ Martin Luther King Jr. was a Baptist minister.

- Ⓑ He also wanted the government to help poor Americans of all colors.

- Ⓒ The reason was to demand equal justice for African Americans.

- Ⓓ He led the civil rights movement from the mid-1950s until his assassination in 1968.

30 Which of these would be a good title for the time line?

- Ⓐ *Important Events of the 1960s*

- Ⓑ *Settling the Colonies*

- Ⓒ *Martin Luther King Jr.'s Fight for Civil Rights*

- Ⓓ *African Americans: From Slavery to Freedom*

Fossils

JEFFREY JUNG / SHUTTERSTOCK

Scientists study the fossils in rocks to find out how old the rocks are. Fossils give clues about what happened in Earth's history. Fossils are mainly found in rock that used to be mud millions of years ago. Most fossils are the remains of animals and plants from the distant past. Some fossils are so small that they must be studied under a microscope. These are the kind that scientists study the most.

STYVE REINECK / SHUTTERSTOCK

A dinosaur fossil

The word *fossil* makes many people think of dinosaurs. The bones and large fossils of some dinosaurs are in many museums. These reptiles lived on Earth for more than 100 million years. Some dinosaurs were quite small. But some weighed as much as 80 tons (72,574.8 kg)! Around 65 million years ago, all dinosaurs became extinct. No one really knows why they disappeared so quickly.

PHOTOS.COM

William Smith

At one time, scientists did not know which fossils came first. They did not know which animals in fossils were older than others. Someone who helped make this clear was William Smith. He was an English engineer. Smith was in charge of building waterways in England about 100 years ago. He needed to know what kinds of rocks to cut through in the hills. Often, he could tell if the rock under the ground was hard or soft. He did this by studying fossils lying nearby.

Smith knew it was useful to tell how and when rocks were formed. But it wasn't until much later that scientists could explain what fossils tell us about Earth's history. They continue to learn about Earth's history by putting fossils in order, from the oldest ones to the most recent.

Previewing

PART 1

Directions: Write what you can learn from the picture your teacher showed you. Then write what you will read about.

_____

_____

_____

PART 2

Directions: Write a sentence that tells what you think this passage will be about. Then draw a picture of your prediction.

_____

PART 3

Directions: Write a sentence telling what kind of text this is. Then write a sentence about what kind of information you will learn.

_____

_____

Previewing *(cont.)*

Directions: Write the important words that help you understand this passage. Then draw pictures of them.

Key words: _____

Directions: Tell someone about the book you chose. Then answer the questions below.

1. What is the title? _____

2. What clues does it give you about the book? _____

   _____

3. What kind of text is it? Is it a letter? A list? A poem? Something else?

   _____

4. What do you see in the pictures? What does that tell you about the text?

   _____

   _____

   _____

Name _____

Comprehension Review

Directions: Fill in the best answer for each question.

1 This is probably a

- Ⓐ letter to the editor.
- Ⓑ diary entry.
- Ⓒ section from a nonfiction book.
- Ⓓ set of instructions.

2 The title tells you this will probably be about

- Ⓐ how to do an experiment.
- Ⓑ pioneer life.
- Ⓒ someone's life.
- Ⓓ fossils.

3 Which topic will probably **not** be in this passage?

- Ⓐ how to become a scientist
- Ⓑ what fossils tell us
- Ⓒ what scientists do with fossils
- Ⓓ studying fossils

4 Fossils are mainly found

- Ⓐ by William Smith.
- Ⓑ in rock that used to be mud.
- Ⓒ in England.
- Ⓓ in mud.

5 What is another good title for this passage?

- Ⓐ Fossils and Dinosaurs: What's the Difference?
- Ⓑ How Old Are Rocks?
- Ⓒ Fossils: Clues to Earth's History
- Ⓓ The Man Who Discovered Fossils

6 Someday, it will be true that

- Ⓐ there will be fossils from our time.
- Ⓑ all fossils will be destroyed.
- Ⓒ William Smith will discover new fossils.
- Ⓓ fossils will not tell us anything.

Name _____

Written Response

Directions: Imagine that you are talking to a friend who doesn't know anything about fossils. What would you tell him or her? Write a letter that includes the most important information that you want to share with your friend. Be sure to include details from the passage.

Saved By the Bell

The mice could stand it no longer. From everywhere in the house, they gathered in the Great Hall of Discussion, which was really the old broom closet in the basement by the water heater. What was the reason for their meeting? What were they upset about? They needed to decide what to do about their great enemy, the cat!

"That cat is so dangerous; she'll destroy hundreds of us!" shouted one mouse angrily.

"Thousands!" agreed another.

"Order! Order!" demanded a fat mouse with a long tail. He drummed his foot thunderously on the water heater to get everyone's attention.

"Ahem!" he began at last, when all the mice had settled down. From the corner of the basement, a cricket watched with interest. "We are here to discuss what to do about the cat," said the fat mouse.

"She must be stopped!" squeaked a frightened voice. It came from a young mouse who had barely escaped the cat's claws—claws that were as sharp as fishhooks.

"I agree," said the fat mouse. "We need protection from her. But what can we do?"

"I know!" cried one of the mice. He was thin and nervous-looking. He had not dared to steal food from the kitchen for three weeks. "The cat is deadly because we can't hear her coming. We need to be able to hear her, you see?" The mice all nodded in agreement.

"But how? What can we do to make the cat louder?" questioned the fat mouse.

"Tie a bell around her!" replied the thin mouse excitedly. "A bell on a collar around her neck—so that every time she tries to sneak up on us, we'll hear the bell!" The mice looked at each other and cheered. This was the best idea anyone ever had for dealing with the cat. A bell! It was perfect! They jumped up and down. The blue flame under the water heater made their shadows as big as kangaroos on the basement wall. The only mouse who wasn't overjoyed was an old mouse who shook his head sadly.

"All right, it's settled," said the fat mouse. "We'll tie a bell around the cat's neck, and we won't need to be afraid of her anymore. Now, who will volunteer to put the bell on the cat?"

Silence. Most of the mice looked down, hoping not to be noticed. Finally, the old mouse spoke up. "Yes, it's easy to talk about an idea, but acting on it is another story!"

Name _____

Cause and Effect—Plot

PART 1

Directions: Tell what happened. Write the effect for each cause in the T-chart below.

Cause	Effect
1. I lost my wallet.	1.
2. I forgot my homework at school.	2.
3. It rained all weekend.	3.

PART 2

Directions: Fill in the chart below with the correct cause or effect.

Cause	Effect
1.	1. The mice had a meeting.
2. The cat was very quiet.	2.
3.	3. The mice cheered.
4. The fat mouse asked, "Who will volunteer to put the bell on the cat?"	4.

PART 3

Directions: Write a sentence that tells about a cause and effect from the passage. Use your own words. Then draw a picture to go with your sentence.

_____

Cause and Effect—Plot (cont.)

PART 4

Directions: List key words from the story that tell you about causes and effects.

Key words: _____

_____

_____

PART 5

Directions: Write your prediction about what will happen next in the story. Be sure to say why you made that prediction.

_____

_____

_____

_____

Name _____

Comprehension Review

Directions: Fill in the best answer for each question.

1 What caused the cat to be so deadly?

Ⓐ The cat stole the mice's food.

Ⓑ The cat was so quiet that the mice couldn't hear her coming.

Ⓒ The cat kept stepping on the mice.

Ⓓ The cat made too much noise.

2 What was the effect of the blue flame under the water heater?

Ⓐ It made the room too hot.

Ⓑ It told the mice where the cat was.

Ⓒ It made the mice's shadows big.

Ⓓ It had no effect.

3 What made the old mouse shake his head sadly?

Ⓐ He knew the mice would not put a bell on the cat.

Ⓑ He was afraid of the other mice.

Ⓒ He was hungry.

Ⓓ He was too tired to stay awake.

4 Which is an example of a simile?

Ⓐ From the corner of the basement, a cricket watched with interest.

Ⓑ He drummed his foot thunderously on the water heater.

Ⓒ The blue flame under the water heater made their shadows as big as kangaroos.

Ⓓ "Every time she tries to sneak up on us, we'll hear the bell!"

5 From whose point of view is the story told?

Ⓐ the mice

Ⓑ the cricket

Ⓒ the cat

Ⓓ the bell

6 What is the setting of the story?

Ⓐ the kitchen

Ⓑ the basement

Ⓒ around a campfire

Ⓓ long ago

Name _____

Written Response

Directions: Think about the cause-and-effect relationship in the passage: the mice fear the cat, so they make a plan to lessen their fears. What do you the think the effect of the plan will be? Will they be able to get a bell onto the cat? If so, what will happen? Include specific examples to support your response.

Oysterville Crate Race

Can you walk on water?

Well, maybe you can by stepping on a row of wooden crates. The Oysterville Crate Race is a crazy way to take a swim, but a great way to have some fun!

Prizes

- First place in each age group wins $25.
- Runner-up in each age group wins an oyster dinner.

MIKHAIL RULKOV / SHUTTERSTOCK

Who Can Enter?

Boys and Girls:

- **Group 1:** ages 10 and under
- **Group 2:** ages 11 and older

When Is It?

August 15th

Where Is It?

Clear Lake Landing

Rules for the Race

For the race, 50 wooden crates are tied together between two piers. The crates float on top of the water, and racers try to balance themselves while they run across the crates as fast as possible. If they make it across all 50 crates, they must turn around and race back across them. The object is to cross as many times as possible without falling off.

What You Need

- sneakers
- a bathing suit
- good balance

Name _____

Headings to Determine Main Ideas

PART 1

Directions: Write why you think the author included headings in this passage.

_____

_____

PART 2

Directions: Use the headings from the passage to answer the questions below.

1. When is the Oysterville Crate Race?_____

2. What three things do you need to compete in this event?

    _____

3. What is the first-place prize? _____

4. What is the rule if you "make it across the crates"?

    _____

PART 3

Directions: Answer the questions below.

1. What is the main idea of the "Rules for the Race" section?

    _____

    _____

2. Which section's main idea is that boys and girls of different ages may enter the contest?

    _____

Name _____

Headings to Determine Main Ideas *(cont.)*

PART 4

Directions: Use the headings below to answer the questions.

"Class Location, Dates, and Times"   "What to Practice at Home"

"Dog Requirements"   "Praising Your Dog"

"Training Tips"   "Doggie Graduation"

---

1. I want to know whether to give my dog a treat after he obeys. Where should I look for information? _____

2. I want to know what training tips will be learned in the class. What is the heading for the section I should read? _____

3. Where should I look to know what time class starts? _____

4. My dog is two months old. May I bring him to class? Where should I look to find out? _____ _____

5. I hear there is a party to celebrate all that the dogs learn in the class. Where should I look to read about this? _____

PART 5

Directions: Choose a book with headings. Then answer the questions below.

1. What is the title of your book?

   _____

2. What are two of the headings you found in the book?

   _____

3. How could you use these headings to help you as you read?

   _____

Name _____

Comprehension Review

Directions: Fill in the best answer for each question.

1 Which heading would you use to find out what you need to bring to the race?

- Ⓐ Prizes
- Ⓑ Who Can Enter?
- Ⓒ When Is It?
- Ⓓ What You Need

2 Where will you find information about who can race?

- Ⓐ What You Need
- Ⓑ Who Can Enter?
- Ⓒ Rules for the Race
- Ⓓ Where Is It?

3 Which information will you probably find under the heading "Rules for the Race?"

- Ⓐ where the race will be
- Ⓑ who may enter the race
- Ⓒ what the rules of the race are
- Ⓓ what the prizes are

4 Why might you read this information?

- Ⓐ to find out when and where something will happen
- Ⓑ to learn about Oysterville
- Ⓒ to learn about someone's life
- Ⓓ to learn about how crates are made

5 Why would you need a bathing suit to enter the crate race?

- Ⓐ Bathing suits are less expensive than other clothes.
- Ⓑ Bathing suits match the crates better than other clothes.
- Ⓒ Bathing suits help you run faster.
- Ⓓ The crates float on water, and you might fall into the water.

6 A person who likes _____ would probably be interested in this.

- Ⓐ cooking
- Ⓑ animals
- Ⓒ outdoor games
- Ⓓ computer games

Written Response

Directions: Think about how the headings in the passage helped you understand what you read. Create an event poster. Be sure to include the proper headings and details for your readers.

George Washington Carver

George Washington Carver never knew his parents. His mother was taken by slave raiders when he was an infant. His father died in a farming accident shortly before his mother was taken. For most of his youth, George was raised by a white couple. They were the Carvers, and they lived in Diamond Grove, Missouri.

When Carver was 12, he tried to find a school that would allow blacks to attend. His travels took him to Missouri, Iowa, and Kansas. He earned money by working as a farmhand, cook, and laundry helper.

In 1894, Carver graduated with honors from Iowa State College. He took a job there as the director of the greenhouse. During this time, he discovered a new kind of fungus plant. It grows on the leaves of red and silver maple trees. Many people started to find out about Carver's work in agriculture.

Then Tuskegee Institute opened its doors to black students. Carver was asked to head the Department of Agriculture. Not only did he do research, but he was also in charge of teaching the farmers. They had been planting cotton for years. But the soil lacked nutrients. To make matters worse, the boll weevil had destroyed acres of cotton. Carver told them to plant goobers—what we now know as peanuts—as an alternative crop.

George Washington Carver

Carver's soybean lab

That season produced more than enough peanuts. In fact, no one knew what to do with all of them. So, Carver went to work in his lab. He began analyzing the peanut. He found that he could take out a substance similar to cow's milk and make cheese from it. After mashing peanuts, he was able to use the oil to make cooking oil, soap, and body oil. And, of course, peanut butter. Overall, he discovered more than 300 products that could be made from peanuts.

George Washington Carver died on January 5, 1943. He was buried on the campus of Tuskegee Institute. Five years later, the United States honored him by putting his picture on a three-cent postage stamp.

Name _____

Main Idea

Directions: Your teacher read the passage aloud and shared thoughts about the main idea. Write what you think the main idea of the passage is.

_____

_____

Directions: Think about the main idea you wrote in Part 1. Now fill in the supporting details for the main idea you have identified.

Supporting detail: _____

Supporting detail: _____

Supporting detail: _____

Supporting detail: _____

Directions: Sketch a graphic organizer in the box below. Fill it in with ideas from the passage you just read.

Name _____

Main Idea *(cont.)*

PART 4

Directions: Write a short paragraph that includes at least four supporting details. The first sentence, or main idea, has been written for you.

Reading every day is one of the most important things you can do to be a good student in school.

_____

_____

_____

_____

PART 5

Directions: Share your work in Part 4 with a partner. Then answer the questions below.

1. Who is your partner? _____

2. What details supported the main idea?

   Detail #1: _____

   Detail #2: _____

   Detail #3: _____

   Detail #4: _____

3. Was your partner's writing clear and organized?

   _____

Comprehension Review

Directions: Fill in the best answer for each question.

1 Which one would be another good title for this passage?

(A) The Story of the Peanut

(B) The Tuskegee Institute

(C) The Life of George Washington Carver

(D) How to Make Cooking Oil

2 This is **mostly** a

(A) biography of George Washington Carver.

(B) recipe for making peanut oil.

(C) history of African Americans.

(D) time line of the American Revolution.

3 Which sentence tells the main idea of this passage?

(A) George Washington Carver lived at the end of the nineteenth century.

(B) George Washington Carver learned many uses for the peanut.

(C) George Washington Carver was the son of slaves.

(D) George Washington Carver was a former slave who became a scientist and an educator.

4 What was one of the primary problems that Carver found with the soil?

(A) There was too much rain.

(B) The boll weevil had destroyed acres of land.

(C) The farmers did not know how to grow cotton.

(D) The farmers had planted too much cotton.

5 What was George Washington Carver's solution to the problem of poor soil?

(A) planting peanuts

(B) adding water to the soil

(C) growing more cotton

(D) adding more sand to the soil

6 George Washington Carver probably liked to read books about

(A) sports.

(B) science.

(C) travel.

(D) Hollywood stars.

Name _____

Written Response

Directions: The passage you read about George Washington Carver included many details about his life. Think about the main idea of the passage. Write the main idea and then explain how it helped you better understand what you read.

A group of zebras in the African grasslands

Sand dunes in the Sahara

A Look at Africa

African Grasslands

Tall, thin grasses rustle and sway in the breeze. A herd of zebras runs through the stalks in graceful bounds. In the distance, an elephant's trumpet sounds. This is the world of the grasslands. One of the most beautiful and famous of the grassland areas is the Serengeti Plain. It is found in Tanzania, a country in eastern Africa.

The Serengeti is usually warm and dry. But it does rain from March to May and a little during October and November. In the Serengeti, it is coldest from June to October.

The most important feature of grasslands is that they are covered with grass all year long. Grasslands also have trees and bushes, but they are scattered and spread apart. Types of trees that grow in the grasslands include palm, pine, and acacia.

The grasses, bushes, and trees are important for animals. Many of them eat these plants for food. Water is also important for all living things. Because of wet and dry seasons and baking from the sun, the soil in some areas of the grasslands hardens. When it rains, the water does not soak into the ground. Instead, it may pool up for many months, providing water for the animals.

The Sahara

The Sahara is the largest hot desert in the world. It covers most of North Africa. More than 25 percent of the Sahara is covered by sheets of sand and sand dunes. The rest is made up of mountains, stony steppes, and oases. Sand dunes are hills or ridges of sand piled up by the wind. Some sand dunes and ridges get to be 500 to 1,000 feet (152.5 to 304.8 m) high!

The Sahara is very dry, but there is an annual rainfall in most regions. Half of the Sahara receives less than an inch (2.5 cm) of rain a year. The rest of it receives up to 3.9 inches (9.9 cm) a year. The northern and southern parts of the Sahara have slightly different climates. But summers are hot all over the desert. The highest temperature ever recorded was 136°F (57.7°C) in Lybia.

Animal life in the Sahara mainly includes gazelles, antelopes, jackals, foxes, badgers, and hyenas. Plant life includes grasses, shrubs, and trees in the highlands and in the oases along the riverbeds.

Name _____

Compare and Contrast

PART 1

Directions: Think about dogs and cats. Then answer the questions below.

1. How are they the same? _____

2. How are they different? _____

PART 2

Directions: Think about the similarities and differences between the African grasslands and the Sahara. Fill in the Venn diagram below. Write similarities in the center, where the ovals overlap. Write differences in the outer parts of the ovals.

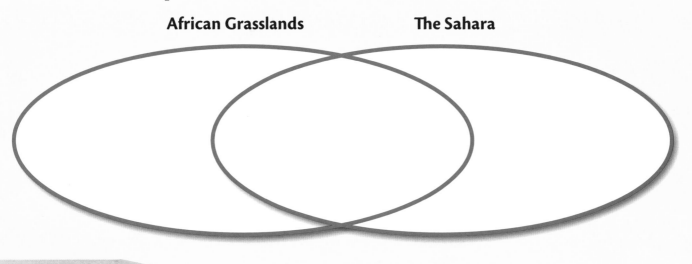

African Grasslands   **The Sahara**

PART 3

Directions: Answer the questions below.

1. What is the difference between the geography of the African grasslands and the Sahara?

    _____

2. What is the name of the most well-known grassland area in Africa?

    _____

3. List one reason you would want to visit either of the places in the passage.

    _____

Name _____

Compare and Contrast *(cont.)*

PART 4

Directions: Reread the passage. You learned that there are many words that help you find a compare-and-contrast relationship. Rewrite two sentences from the passage using these words.

1. _____

    _____

2. _____

    _____

PART 5

Directions: Fill in the information below. Then use the information to fill in the Venn diagram, comparing your information to your partner's information.

> I have _____ brothers or sisters. My favorite color is
> _____. I have _____ colored eyes. I have
> _____ colored hair. My favorite food is _____.
> My favorite subject in school is _____. My favorite game to
> play is _____.

Name:_____   **Both**   **Name:** _____

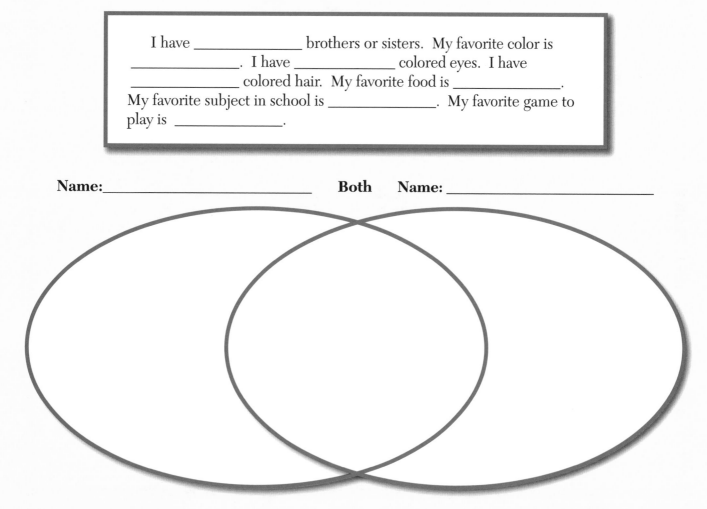

Name _____

Comprehension Review

Directions: Fill in the best answer for each question.

1 The African grasslands and the Sahara are both usually

  Ⓐ full of sand dunes.

  Ⓑ covered by grass.

  Ⓒ rainy.

  Ⓓ dry.

2 Unlike the Sahara, the grasslands

  Ⓐ are covered with grass all year long.

  Ⓑ get rain all year long.

  Ⓒ have oases along riverbeds.

  Ⓓ have only pine trees.

3 Animals more common to the grasslands than the Sahara are

  Ⓐ gazelles and badgers.

  Ⓑ foxes and antelopes.

  Ⓒ zebras and elephants.

  Ⓓ zebras and hyenas.

4 The author wrote this

  Ⓐ to tell about the history of Africa.

  Ⓑ to tell about different parts of Africa.

  Ⓒ to tell a story about Africa.

  Ⓓ to get you to visit Africa.

5 About how much of the Sahara is covered by sand?

  Ⓐ 39 percent

  Ⓑ 15 percent

  Ⓒ 58 percent

  Ⓓ 25 percent

6 If you did not remember when the Serengeti gets rain, what could you do?

  Ⓐ Write the words.

  Ⓑ Look at the title.

  Ⓒ Read the paragraph again.

  Ⓓ Read about annual rainfall.

Name _____

Written Response

Directions: Briefly describe the similarities and differences between the African grasslands and the Sahara. Then choose a place that you have visited and tell how it is similar or different from the places in the passage.

KAREN LOWE

The Lion and the Mouse

From Aesop's Fables, by Aesop

Once, when a lion was asleep, a little mouse began running up and down the lion's back. This soon caused the lion to wake up. He then placed his huge paw upon the mouse and opened his big jaws to swallow him. "Pardon, O King," cried the little mouse. "Forgive me this time—I shall never forget your mercy. Who knows when I may be able to return the favor?" The lion was tickled at the idea of the little mouse helping a huge lion like him someday. So, he lifted up his paw and let him go.

Some time later, the lion got caught in a trap. The hunters who caught the lion desired to take him alive to the king. So, they tied him to a tree while they went in search of a wagon to carry him.

Just then, the little mouse happened to pass by. Seeing the sad situation that the lion was in, the mouse went up to him and gnawed through the ropes that bound the king of the beasts. "Was I not right?" said the little mouse.

The moral of this fable is: Little friends may prove to be great friends.

Name _____

Selecting Reading Material

PART 1

Directions: Write two sentences about the kinds of books you like to read.

_____

_____

PART 2

Directions: Write a sentence about what kind of story "The Lion and the Mouse" is. Then draw a picture from the story.

_____

PART 3

Directions: Tell whether you would recommend this passage to someone else. Explain why or why not.

_____

_____

_____

Selecting Reading Material *(cont.)*

PART 4

Directions: Work with a partner. Find out what your partner's interests or hobbies are, and then recommend a book for him or her.

1. My partner is _____ .

2. My partner likes _____ .

3. I recommend this book to my partner: _____

    _____

PART 5

Directions: Fill in the information below.

1. Who is your favorite author? _____

2. What do you like about your favorite author's work?

    _____

    _____

3. Name a book or story by this author.

    _____

4. Why would you recommend this book or story?

    _____

    _____

Comprehension Review

Directions: Fill in the best answer for each question.

1 _____ would like to read this.

Ⓐ An animal lover

Ⓑ Someone who likes science

Ⓒ An artist

Ⓓ A person who likes gardening

2 This would **not** be a good choice for someone who

Ⓐ is interested in friendship.

Ⓑ likes reading about animals.

Ⓒ loves to read about sports.

Ⓓ enjoys reading fiction.

3 People who like _____ would want to read this.

Ⓐ mysteries

Ⓑ poetry

Ⓒ biographies

Ⓓ fables

4 *I shall never forget your mercy.*

The mouse says this to the lion because

Ⓐ he is upset with the lion for catching him.

Ⓑ he is grateful that the lion didn't eat him.

Ⓒ he wants to trick the lion.

Ⓓ he is usually forgetful.

5 Why does the lion decide to let the mouse go?

Ⓐ He is amused by the idea that the mouse could return the favor.

Ⓑ He wants to be friends with the mouse.

Ⓒ He is promised a prize for letting the mouse go.

Ⓓ He is annoyed by the mouse.

6 How does the mouse help the lion when he is caught by hunters?

Ⓐ He doesn't help the lion.

Ⓑ He distracts the hunters.

Ⓒ He convinces the hunters to let the lion go.

Ⓓ He gnaws through the ropes that bind the lion.

Name _____

Written Response

Directions: Tell what you think the purpose of a fable is. Then explain why someone might choose to read a fable. Include several examples to support your response.

MAGDALENA BUJAK / SHUTTERSTOCK

GEORGE PAPPAS / SHUTTERSTOCK

ADMIT ONE

The Special Gift

It was Valentine's Day. For the first time, there were two gifts waiting for me on the kitchen counter—one from my mother and one from my father. Instead of being happy, my heart ached.

I had just been to a friend's birthday party where I watched her unwrap a special gift her father had picked up for her. For me, this was unusual. My mother did all of the special occasion shopping. All my dad did was sign his name on the card, or my mother did it for him. When I confronted my dad about this after the party, he didn't say a word. He left the room. My mother cast her disapproving shadow across the room and stated, "I'm disappointed in you. We're a family. How could you hurt your father like that?"

It may sound silly, but when I saw my friend open up her present from her father, I wanted that moment. I wanted my father to want that moment.

My mother's card to me was beautiful, as always. I knew she had looked over every card in the stationery store and selected this one just for me. In the envelope were two movie passes—one for her and one for me. Mother was so thoughtful.

As always, I expected my dad's card to be corny—but it wasn't. On the front was a picture of a carousel. I sensed my father had thoughtfully chosen this card, because it didn't seem like a regular Valentine card. When I opened it, I knew I was right. There was no machine-scribed message inside. My eyes misted as I read my father's handwritten message.

Wrapped in tissue paper was a small tin of sugar-covered lemon drops. They were my dad's favorite, but he used to share them with me. I wondered where he got them. I placed a lemon drop on my tongue and closed my eyes. I desperately tried to remember the rides on the carousel with my father, just as he described them in his message.

I went to put the tin and card in my memory box. When I pulled the box out from under my bed, it tipped and a red ticket stub fluttered out. When I held it in my hand, I remembered. I remembered the tinny music, the grasp of my five fingers around my father's hand, and the ponies that brought children to their destination. I remembered holding so tightly to the ticket, afraid it would blow away in the wind and I'd miss my special time with my dad. I smiled. I knew my father would never have let that happen—not in the past, and not in the present or future.

Name _____

Character Development

PART 1

Directions: Write a few words to describe the narrator.

_____

_____

PART 2

Directions: Make a list of the other characters in the story. Then write a word that describes each character.

Character's Name	Description

PART 3

Directions: Write about two things that caused the narrator to change.

_____

_____

_____

_____

Name _____

Character Development (cont.)

Directions: Think about which character besides the narrator is the most important. Tell why you think that character is important.

_____

_____

_____

Directions: Write a dialogue between the narrator and the character you chose in Part 4. What would these characters say to each other?

_____

_____

_____

_____

_____

_____

_____

_____

Name _____

Comprehension Review

Directions: Fill in the best answer for each question.

1 Which is a good word to describe the narrator at the beginning of the story?

ⓐ happy

ⓑ terrified

ⓒ sad

ⓓ nervous

2 Why did the narrator's eyes get misty when she opened her dad's card?

ⓐ It had a picture of a carousel in it.

ⓑ It had a personal handwritten message inside.

ⓒ It was the first card he had ever given her.

ⓓ It was corny and impersonal.

3 Which sentence **best** shows how the narrator feels about her dad at the end of the story?

ⓐ I wanted my father to want that moment.

ⓑ I expected my dad's card to be corny.

ⓒ Instead of being happy, my heart ached.

ⓓ I smiled. I knew my father would never let that happen.

4 What is the second special gift that the narrator got from her father?

ⓐ a tin of sugar-covered lemon drops

ⓑ a carousel figurine

ⓒ a memory box

ⓓ movie passes for the two of them

5 At first, how were gifts from the narrator's mother different than those from her father?

ⓐ They were expensive.

ⓑ They were thoughtful.

ⓒ They were large.

ⓓ They were fun.

6 What caused the narrator to remember rides on the carousel with her father?

ⓐ her Valentine's Day card

ⓑ a small tin of lemon drops

ⓒ a red ticket stub

ⓓ her memory box

Written Response

Directions: Think about how the narrator and her father changed throughout the story. Write about a time when you had a similar experience with a friend or family member. Tell how you changed as a result of the experience.

Who Was George Washington?

George Washington was an important man in American history. He was a hero in the French and Indian War. He led soldiers in the American Revolution. Then, Washington became the first president of a new country.

George Washington was born in Westmoreland County, Virginia. His father died when he was 11. So, he moved in with his brother Lawrence. Lawrence owned a large farm in Virginia called Mount Vernon.

At age 16, Washington became a surveyor of land. He helped measure and map new towns in western Virginia.

When Lawrence died, Washington inherited Mount Vernon. This plantation became his home for many years.

After the Revolutionary War, people knew that Washington was a great leader. So, he was elected as the first president of the United States.

Washington believed the country had to have a strong government to be powerful. He asked for help as president. He called his assistants the *cabinet*.

George Washington became the first president of the United States.

Mount Vernon, George Washington's plantation

Washington became upset with the U.S. Congress. He thought that Congress took too long to make laws. He said he would never go to Congress again. Instead, he would just write letters to them. U.S. presidents still write letters to Congress today.

People wanted Washington to be president for a long time. He did not want to be a dictator, so he stepped down after eight years.

Washington moved back to Mount Vernon. He was happy to be home with his wife, Martha. One day, Washington was riding his horse. He became sick with chills and a sore throat. He died that night, on December 14, 1799. He is buried at Mount Vernon.

Topic Sentences to Determine Main Ideas

PART 1

Directions: Think about the first sentence of this passage:

George Washington was an important man in American history.

What information do you expect to read about in this text? Write your ideas below.

_____

_____

PART 2

Directions: A topic sentence tells a reader what a paragraph or section of text will be about. Find two topic sentences in this passage and record them below.

1. _____

   _____

2. _____

   _____

PART 3

Directions: Read the story below. It is missing a topic sentence. Write one that would fit as the first sentence in this story.

> During autumn, leaves are changing colors and falling to the ground. When winter comes around, snow blankets the ground, and temperatures drop so that the air feels icy cold. Spring brings new life to our town, and flowers bloom in the sunshine. Finally, during summer, the sun comes out each day, and the heat feels warm on your skin. Which season do you like best?

Topic sentence:_____

_____

Topic Sentences to Determine Main Ideas *(cont.)*

PART 4

Directions: Write a paragraph below. Remember to include a topic sentence.

_____

_____

_____

_____

_____

_____

PART 5

Directions: Share your work in Part 4 with a partner. Write the topic sentence from your partner's paragraph.

_____

_____

Comprehension Review

Directions: Fill in the best answer for each question.

1 *Washington became upset with the U.S. Congress.*

Which detail tells you more about this topic sentence?

- Ⓐ He was happy to be home with his wife, Martha.
- Ⓑ He called his assistants the *cabinet*.
- Ⓒ His father died when he was 11.
- Ⓓ He thought that Congress took too long to make laws.

2 Which one is **not** a topic sentence?

- Ⓐ George Washington was an important man in American history.
- Ⓑ Washington became upset with the U.S. Congress.
- Ⓒ He asked for help as president.
- Ⓓ At age 16, Washington became a surveyor of land.

3 Which sentence tells the main idea of this passage?

- Ⓐ George Washington was an important man in American history.
- Ⓑ Washington became upset with Congress.
- Ⓒ At age 16, Washington became a surveyor of land.
- Ⓓ Washington moved back to Mount Vernon.

4 The author probably thinks that

- Ⓐ Washington was not a good soldier.
- Ⓑ Washington wanted to be a dictator.
- Ⓒ we should not remember who George Washington was.
- Ⓓ Washington was a great president.

5 What caused Washington to step down after eight years as president?

- Ⓐ Congress asked him to step down.
- Ⓑ He did not want to be a dictator.
- Ⓒ His wife, Martha, asked him to step down.
- Ⓓ Washington was tired of being president.

6 How could you tell someone else what this passage is about?

- Ⓐ This is about George Washington, who was a surveyor, a war hero, and the first U.S. president.
- Ⓑ This is about how George Washington became a surveyor.
- Ⓒ This is about how the U.S. Congress makes laws.
- Ⓓ This is about how George Washington became president.

Name _____

Written Response

Directions: Write a summary of the passage on George Washington. Use the topic sentences and details from the passage. Remember to include only the most important information.

An Amazing Machine

Your body is an amazing machine. A machine has many parts that work together to make it run. In much the same way, a human has body systems that work together to keep a person alive. One system is not more important than another. All are necessary in order for the body to live. Two body systems that work together are the circulatory system and the respiratory system.

The Circulatory System

The circulatory system moves blood throughout the body. Your cells need a constant supply of fresh blood. Blood has red blood cells, white blood cells, and platelets. The red blood cells carry oxygen from the lungs to the rest of the body. They also bring back carbon dioxide and waste. White blood cells attack germs to keep the body healthy. Platelets stop bleeding by forming clots. Without platelets, you could bleed to death from a small cut!

The heart is the pump of the circulatory system. Your heart is about the size of your fist. This muscle pumps blood through blood vessels. Actually, the heart has two pumps. The heart's left pump gets blood from the lungs. This blood has oxygen. The heart pumps it to cells all over the body. The heart's right pump gets the blood returning from the cells. This blood has carbon dioxide in it. The right pump moves this blood to the lungs. There, the carbon dioxide is taken out of the blood and oxygen is added.

ILLUSTRATION BY RICK NEASE

The Respiratory System

The respiratory system gives the body oxygen and gets rid of carbon dioxide. When you inhale, your lungs get bigger, and oxygen rushes into them. When you exhale, your chest gets smaller, pushing carbon dioxide out. Air enters through the nose or mouth. Inside your nose are millions of tiny hairs. These hairs trap dust and dirt so that mostly clean air goes down the trachea, or windpipe, to the lungs. Right above the lungs, the windpipe splits into two tubes. One tube enters each lung.

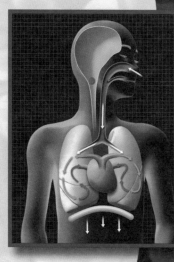

Inside the lungs, these tubes branch into many smaller tubes. These smaller tubes have millions of air sacs. Carbon dioxide and oxygen are exchanged in these air sacs. Carbon dioxide leaves the blood and goes into the air sacs. Then oxygen moves through the air sacs into the blood. This oxygen-filled blood goes to the heart. The carbon dioxide leaves the lungs with the next exhale.

ILLUSTRATION BY RICK NEASE

Name _____

Prior Knowledge

PART 1

Directions: Fill in the word web with things that you know about the heart.

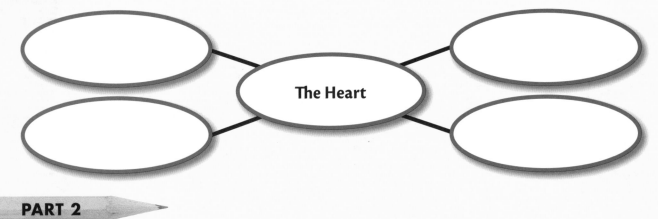

PART 2

Directions: Fill in the word web with things that you know about how we breathe.

PART 3

Directions: Write two things that you have learned about each system.

Circulatory system:_____

_____

_____

Respiratory system: _____

_____

_____

Prior Knowledge *(cont.)*

PART 4

Directions: Imagine telling someone about how the body works. Write a few sentences about the circulatory system and the respiratory system.

_____

_____

_____

_____

PART 5

Directions: Practice using your prior knowledge. Read the text provided by your teacher. Write two pieces of information that you learned.

1. _____

_____

2. _____

_____

Name _____

Comprehension Review

Directions: Fill in the best answer for each question.

1 Knowing what the heart does will help you learn about the _____ system.

   (A) trachea

   (B) circulatory

   (C) respiratory

   (D) carbon dioxide

2 If you think about _____, it is easier to learn about platelets.

   (A) air sacs

   (B) carbon dioxide

   (C) lungs

   (D) blood

3 You already know about _____. This helps you understand how carbon dioxide and oxygen are exchanged.

   (A) the heart

   (B) blood

   (C) breathing

   (D) the stomach

4 What do platelets do for your body?

   (A) They form clots that stop bleeding.

   (B) They cause the heart to stop working.

   (C) They help you digest food.

   (D) They make new blood cells.

5 To inhale means to

   (A) make oxygen.

   (B) breathe out.

   (C) breathe in.

   (D) pump blood.

6 You would read this passage if you wanted to

   (A) learn how to make something.

   (B) learn about the body's systems.

   (C) read a good mystery.

   (D) read about a famous person.

Written Response

Directions: Think about what you already knew about the human body before reading the passage. Explain how your prior knowledge helped you understand the passage. Then tell a few facts that you learned from reading the passage.

THOMAS JEFFERSON

A lucky little boy named Thomas Jefferson was born in Virginia on April 13, 1743. Jefferson was lucky because his family lived on a beautiful plantation called Shadwell. There was lots of land for him to explore. He rode horses and learned to hunt. He loved the outdoors.

Jefferson was also lucky because he had an excellent mind. He loved to learn. His family hired tutors for him. He read many books each day. He could read in five languages!

Jefferson grew up to be tall and thin. He had red hair and freckles. He was shy and did not talk very much.

When he was almost 17, he went to the College of William and Mary. He was a student there for two years. Jefferson worked very hard. Most days, he studied for 14 hours. He kept notebooks where he wrote down his thoughts about all the things he learned.

Thomas Jefferson

After college, Jefferson studied law for five years. Then he became a lawyer. He traveled all over Virginia. He liked meeting different kinds of people.

Jefferson had many interests besides the law. In fact, it was hard to find a subject that did not interest him. He collected books about many different subjects. He especially loved to read about history, science, nature, and politics.

Many Virginians were unhappy with their leaders in Great Britain. They did not like being told what to do by a king who lived so far away. Jefferson thought that the people should be able to make their own laws. He wrote about this in booklets and newspaper articles. Later, he became the main author of the Declaration of Independence. In 1801, he was elected president of the United States.

Jefferson Memorial

Name _____

Sequential Order

PART 1

Directions: Tell why you think the author chose to write the passage in sequential order.

_____

_____

PART 2

Directions: Make a web of any words or phrases that tell the reader that the passage is written in sequential order.

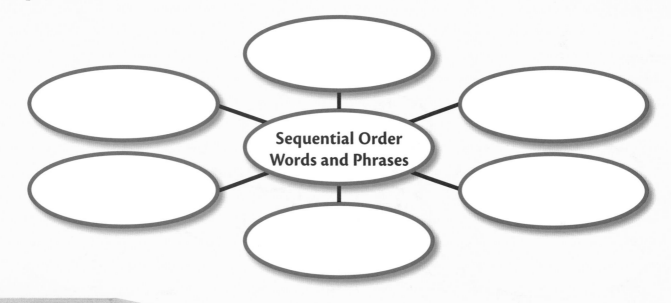

PART 3

Directions: Choose one of the text structures below. Explain how information about Thomas Jefferson might be organized in this new way.

compare and contrast   proposition and support   cause and effect

_____

_____

_____

_____

Name _____

Sequential Order (cont.)

PART 4

Directions: Choose a classroom book with examples of sequential order. Fill in the information below.

Book title: _____

How do you know this story is written in sequential order? _____

_____

_____

PART 5

Directions: Make a web of words or phrases that signal that the text you used in Part 4 is written in sequential order.

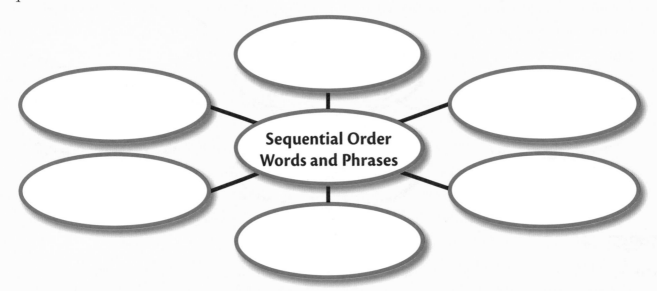

Sequential Order Words and Phrases

Comprehension Review

Directions: Fill in the best answer for each question.

1 Jefferson studied law **before** he

(A) went to the College of William and Mary.

(B) lived at Shadwell.

(C) grew up to be tall and thin.

(D) wrote booklets and newspaper articles.

2 Which did Jefferson do **first**?

(A) He went to the College of William and Mary.

(B) He lived at Shadwell.

(C) He studied law for five years.

(D) He traveled all over Virginia.

3 *Jefferson worked very hard. Most days, he studied for 14 hours.*

What happened **next**?

(A) He went to William and Mary College.

(B) He moved to Shadwell.

(C) He became a lawyer.

(D) He grew up to be tall and thin.

4 Why does the author think that Jefferson was lucky?

(A) He lived on a beautiful plantation and had an excellent mind.

(B) He grew up to be tall and thin.

(C) He went to William and Mary College and worked very hard.

(D) He collected books about many different subjects.

5 What is a plantation?

(A) a kind of car

(B) a large farm where crops are raised

(C) a very large city

(D) the edge of a river

6 Which does **not** support the idea that Jefferson had an excellent mind?

(A) He could read in five languages.

(B) He collected books about many different subjects.

(C) He loved to learn.

(D) He grew up to be tall and thin.

Name _____

Written Response

Directions: Write about the key points and/or events in Thomas Jefferson's life, in the order that they happened. Use details from the passage to support your response.

Earthquakes

When Earth's crust moves and the ground shakes, it is called an earthquake. It can be caused in many ways: Earth's crust may slide, a volcano may become active, or humans may set off an explosion. Earthquakes that cause the most damage result from the crust sliding.

At first, the crust may bend because of pushing forces. When the pushing becomes too intense, the crust snaps and shifts. Shifting creates waves of energy that extend in all directions. These are like the ripples you see when a stone is dropped in water. These are called *seismic waves*. The waves travel out from the center of the earthquake. Sometimes people can hear these waves because they make the whole planet ring like a bell. It is both awesome and frightening to hear this sound!

The crust movement can leave a crack, or fault, in the land. Geologists—scientists who study Earth's surface—say that earthquakes often happen where there are old faults. Wherever there are faults in the crust, it is weaker. This means that earthquakes may happen again and again in that area.

When earthquakes happen under the ocean floor, they sometimes cause huge sea waves. There was an earthquake near Alaska in 1964. Its giant waves caused more damage to some towns than the earthquake did. Some of the waves raced across the ocean in the other direction to the coasts of Japan.

A fault line

LEE PRINCE / SHUTTERSTOCK

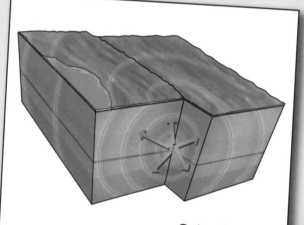

Seismic waves

TIM BRADLEY

USGS

Name _____

Monitoring Reading Strategies

Directions: List some ways that earthquakes can be caused.

_____

_____

_____

Directions: Think about how Earth's crust splits and causes an earthquake. Draw a picture of the crust splitting.

Directions: Tell how an underwater earthquake makes sea waves. Then draw a picture to match.

_____

Name _____

Monitoring Reading Strategies *(cont.)*

PART 4

Directions: List three causes of earthquakes. Then draw pictures to match.

PART 5

Directions: Imagine you are telling someone how to reread or make mental pictures. List the steps to your strategy.

1. _____

2. _____

3. _____

4. _____

Name _____

Comprehension Review

Directions: Fill in the best answer for each question.

1 If you did not remember how an earthquake is caused, what could you do?

- (A) Write the word *earthquake*.
- (B) Read the title.
- (C) Read the first paragraph again.
- (D) Read the last sentence.

2 What is a good way to remember how seismic waves work?

- (A) Write the words.
- (B) Look up the words in a dictionary.
- (C) Read the second paragraph.
- (D) Make a mental picture of a stone dropped into water.

3 *Shifting creates waves of energy that extend in all directions...These are called seismic waves.*

If you wanted to learn more about seismic waves, what could you do?

- (A) Read the rest of the paragraph.
- (B) Look back at the title.
- (C) Read the sentence again.
- (D) Look up the word *earthquake* in a dictionary.

4 Which is an opinion?

- (A) The waves travel out from the center of the earthquake.
- (B) It is both awesome and frightening to hear this sound!
- (C) These are called *seismic waves*.
- (D) There was an earthquake in Alaska in 1964.

5 What is one possible effect of earthquakes?

- (A) a crack that is 3,960 miles long and goes to the center of Earth
- (B) volcanic bursts
- (C) faults, or cracks, in the ground
- (D) a stone dropped in water

6 What would be another good title for this passage?

- (A) Giant Waves from Nowhere
- (B) How Earthquakes Happen
- (C) Stay Put When Earthquakes Happen!
- (D) Earthquakes in Japan

Written Response

Directions: Think about the passage you read on earthquakes. List the words or parts of the passage that you either did not understand or want to know more about. Then use at least one strategy (e.g., reread, look it up) to clarify or get more information. Write your new understanding of the words or parts of the passage.

The Secret to Taking Tests

Kara struggled at school. She did things like pressing too hard on her pencil and breaking it, or losing her schoolwork. It seemed to Kara that she never did anything right. She wondered why she made so many mistakes.

The thing that Kara struggled with the most was her test scores. She usually got the lowest score in class, even though she studied hard. One day after school, she told the teacher how she felt. "Look at my math test. I only got 10 right out of 20 problems," Kara said with a look of disappointment.

"You just don't know the secrets of taking tests," her teacher said.

"There are secrets to taking tests?" asked Kara in surprise. That was the first time she had heard of such a thing.

"Yes, there are, and if you want me to, I will teach them to you." Kara was eager to learn them, so she scooted her chair closer to the teacher's desk.

"The first secret to doing well on tests is getting through the whole test. There were 20 problems on your math test. If you worked hard on the first five and got them all correct, what are the most

points you would score? Yes, five. If you got all the way through 20 problems and even missed 10, what would your score be? Yes, 10. That's twice as many—so it is important to get through the whole test. You do that by following the second secret."

The teacher continued, "The second secret is to do all the easy problems first. You can do this by skipping any problems that look difficult. You can also skip problems that you're not sure how to do. In most tests, you have about one minute for each problem, so skip any problems that take more than a minute to do. If you finish the test and there's still time, go back and finish the problems you skipped."

"Are there any more secrets?" asked Kara.

"Yes," said the teacher. "Ask me about them tomorrow, and I will teach the whole class more test-taking secrets."

Kara was excited. She couldn't wait until the next test. She wanted to try out her new secrets because she wanted to see her test scores go up. Maybe the teacher was right—she really could do it!

Problem and Solution—Plot

PART 1

Directions: Reread the passage aloud and answer the following questions about the characters.

1. Who is the main character? _____

2. How does she feel? _____

3. What makes her feel this way? _____

   _____

4. Who is the other character in the story? _____

PART 2

Directions: Describe the setting of the story.

_____

_____

PART 3

Directions: Write the beginning, middle, and end of the story.

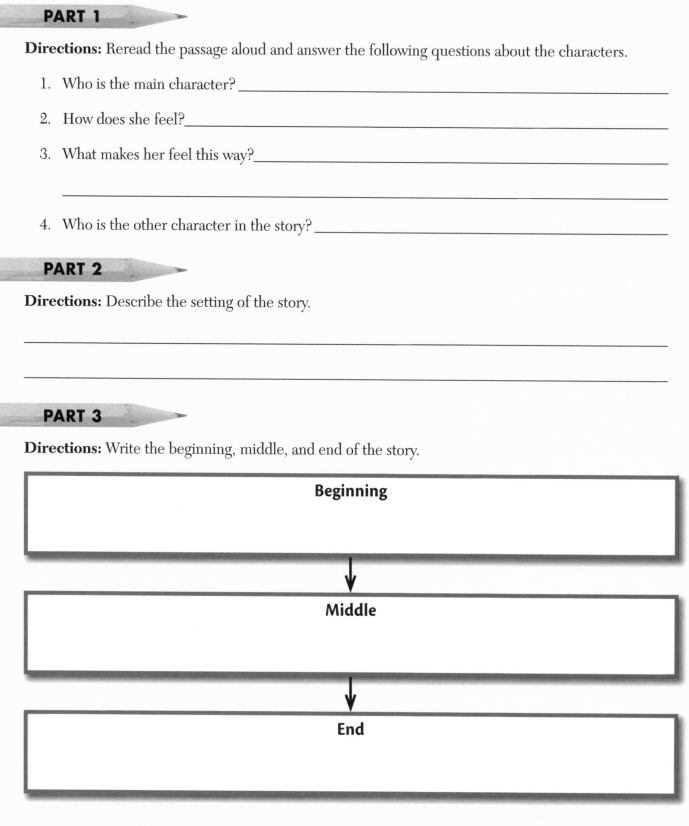

Beginning

↓

Middle

↓

End

Problem and Solution—Plot (cont.)

PART 4

Directions: Answer the following questions.

1. What is the problem in the story? _____

   _____

2. How is it solved? _____

   _____

PART 5

Directions: Write the two secrets that Kara learns about test taking.

_____

_____

_____

_____

Name _____

Comprehension Review

Directions: Fill in the best answer for each question.

1 This story is **mostly** about

   (A) a person.

   (B) a problem and how it was solved.

   (C) a time line of events.

   (D) how two things are alike and different.

2 In the **beginning** of the story, you learn

   (A) where Kara lives.

   (B) how Kara's problem is solved.

   (C) who helps to solve Kara's problem.

   (D) what Kara's problem is.

3 Where can you find the solution to Kara's problem?

   (A) in the middle and end of the story

   (B) in the first sentence of the story

   (C) at the beginning of the story

   (D) by reading the first paragraph

4 When does Kara's point of view about tests change?

   (A) when she asks her parents for help

   (B) when she gets 100% on a test

   (C) when her teacher gives her test-taking secrets

   (D) when she buys a book about taking tests

5 What is the **first** thing that Kara should do when she is taking a test?

   (A) Do the hardest problems.

   (B) Do the easy problems.

   (C) Answer the last question.

   (D) Do the even-numbered problems.

6 Kara is probably _____ that the teacher gave her the secrets to taking tests.

   (A) jealous

   (B) angry

   (C) scared

   (D) grateful

Name _____

Written Response

Directions: Think about a problem you have faced at school. Tell about the problem. Then explain how you solved it.

A carving of Cleopatra, Queen of Egypt, on the side of an ancient Egyptian ruin

CLEOPATRA: QUEEN OF EGYPT

Cleopatra is one of the most famous women in history. She was beautiful and ambitious. Cleopatra lived from 69 to 30 B.C. At the age of 17, she became the queen of Egypt.

While Cleopatra ruled Egypt, Julius Caesar was the emperor of Rome. In 48 B.C., he visited Egypt and fell in love with Cleopatra. When Caesar returned to Rome, Cleopatra traveled with him. However, Caesar was soon killed. So, Cleopatra went back to Egypt alone.

To increase her power, she married a Roman general named Mark Antony. Antony was expected to become the new emperor of Rome. Soon, he started giving away Roman land to his wife. This angered the Roman general named Octavian, so he declared war on Antony and Cleopatra. In a big sea battle, Octavian defeated the Egyptians. Antony killed himself. Cleopatra had lost her power. So, she took her own life as well—by letting a poisonous snake bite her.

Roman Emperor Julius Caesar, who fell in love with Cleopatra

Name _____

Captions to Determine Main Ideas

Directions: Pictures can give the reader a lot of additional information about a topic. Write what you learned about Cleopatra by looking at the pictures.

_____

_____

_____

Directions: Write two things that the picture captions tell you about Cleopatra.

_____

_____

Directions: Use the text provided by your teacher to answer the questions below.

1. Write the picture caption from the text provided by your teacher.

   _____

2. What information does the picture caption provide that cannot be found in the text?

   _____

3. Why is it important to include picture captions?

   _____

Captions to Determine Main Ideas(cont.)

PART 4

Directions: Think about how picture captions help someone reading fiction and nonfiction texts. Fill in the T-chart below.

Fiction	Nonfiction

PART 5

Directions: Write your picture caption in the space below. Then draw a picture to match.

_____

Name _____

Comprehension Review

Directions: Fill in the best answer for each question.

1 The captions tell you that the statue and carving are of

   Ⓐ Cleopatra and her maid.

   Ⓑ Cleopatra and Marc Antony.

   Ⓒ Julius Caesar and Cleopatra.

   Ⓓ Cleopatra and her daughter.

2 The carving of Cleopatra is

   Ⓐ on the side of an Egyptian ruin.

   Ⓑ brand new.

   Ⓒ made of steel.

   Ⓓ too small for most people to see.

3 The caption tells you that Julius Caesar was

   Ⓐ Cleopatra's son.

   Ⓑ a Roman emperor.

   Ⓒ the father of Marc Antony.

   Ⓓ bitten by a snake.

4 People who like to read about _____ would probably like this.

   Ⓐ dinosaurs and fossils

   Ⓑ outer space

   Ⓒ card tricks

   Ⓓ ancient history

5 After Cleopatra went back to Egypt, she

   Ⓐ became queen of Egypt.

   Ⓑ married Julius Caesar.

   Ⓒ married Marc Antony.

   Ⓓ became emperor of Rome.

6 Which one is the topic sentence for this passage?

   Ⓐ Cleopatra is one of the most famous women in history.

   Ⓑ Soon, he started giving away Roman land to his wife.

   Ⓒ When Caesar returned to Rome, Cleopatra traveled with him.

   Ⓓ Octavian defeated the Egyptians.

Written Response

Directions: Look at the pictures and picture captions in this passage about Cleopatra. Tell how they contribute to your understanding of the passage. Be sure to give specific examples to support your response.

The Skeleton and Muscles

Bones are inside every part of your body. Bones connect together to make your skeleton, and your skeleton gives your size and shape. Each bone in your body has its own important job to do. Some bones, such as your skull, protect you. The skull protects your brain. Some bones, such as your ribs, give you shape. Ribs make the shape of your chest and protect your heart, lungs, stomach, and liver. Some bones, such as your femur, or thigh bone, give you strength to stand.

Bones may be soft on the inside, but they are hard on the outside. They are made from some of the same things you can find in rocks! These things are called *minerals*. Bones are also dry compared to the rest of the body. A large part of your body is made of water, but only a small part of your skeleton is.

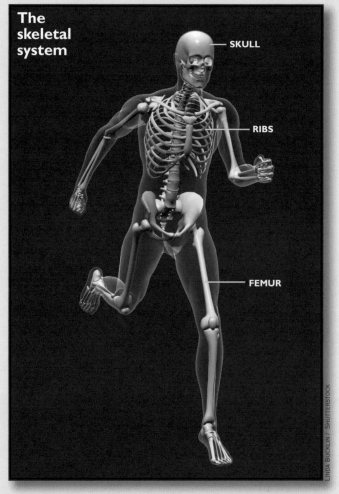

The skeletal system

SKULL

RIBS

FEMUR

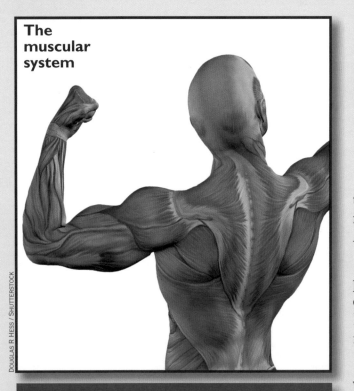

The muscular system

Did you know that it takes more muscles to frown than to smile?

All the bones of your skeleton are connected to each other, except for one. The thyroid bone is in your throat, behind your tongue and above your Adam's apple. Muscles hold it there.

What exactly are muscles? They are the parts of the body that move bones and make body organs such as the heart, lungs, and stomach work. Muscles are also in the walls of blood vessels to make blood move.

There are more than 650 different muscles in your body. Your muscles make up a little less than half your total body weight. So, if you weigh 60 pounds, your muscles weigh about 25 pounds.

Graphic Features

PART 1

Directions: Write a prediction based on the graphic features in the passage.

_____

_____

PART 2

Directions: Write main ideas about the skeleton and the muscles. Use the graphic features to help you.

Main idea about the skeleton: _____

_____

Main idea about the muscles: _____

_____

PART 3

Directions: Explain what each graphic feature tells you.

_____

_____

_____

_____

_____

Name _____

Graphic Features (cont.)

Directions: Create a graphic feature that shows something you learned from the passage.

Directions: Read another text with a graphic feature. Then answer the following questions.

1. What kind of graphic feature did you find (e.g., photo, chart, diagram)?

   _____

2. How did the graphic feature help you as you read?

   _____

   _____

Comprehension Review

Directions: Fill in the best answer for each question.

1 What does the picture of the skeletal system show?

   Ⓐ blood

   Ⓑ the heart

   Ⓒ muscles

   Ⓓ bones

2 What does the picture of the muscular system show?

   Ⓐ leg muscles

   Ⓑ connected muscles

   Ⓒ muscles in blood vessels

   Ⓓ the thyroid bone

3 Look at the picture of the skeletal system. Which is true?

   Ⓐ The leg bones are the longest bones.

   Ⓑ The skull is the smallest bone.

   Ⓒ The neck bones are longer than the leg bones.

   Ⓓ The rib bones are connected to the leg bones.

4 Unlike rib bones, your femur

   Ⓐ protects your stomach.

   Ⓑ is a bone.

   Ⓒ gives you strength to stand.

   Ⓓ is a muscle.

5 What do bones **not** do?

   Ⓐ protect

   Ⓑ make body organs work

   Ⓒ give shape

   Ⓓ give strength

6 Bones and muscles both

   Ⓐ make organs work.

   Ⓑ protect the brain.

   Ⓒ are parts of systems in the body.

   Ⓓ are hard on the outside.

Name _____

Written Response

Directions: Explain how the graphic features helped you understand the passage. Did you learn any information from them? Or, did they just clarify what you read in the passage?

THE GREEK OLYMPICS

In ancient times, athletes arrived in Olympia at least one month prior to the Olympic competitions. During this time, they trained physically and were prepared by priests to become pure in thought and deed. Finally, the games would begin.

DAY ONE: The first day of the Olympic Games was spent in religious worship. Each athlete vowed to compete with true sportsmanship. Animal sacrifices were offered to the god Zeus near his grand temple.

DAY TWO: The second day began with chariot races. Races involved two-wheeled carts drawn by four horses. This was followed by an 800-meter bareback horse race. There were also footraces, wrestling, boxing, and horse racing.

DAY THREE: The third day was devoted to the pentathlon, a grueling test of stamina and skill. Contestants competed in five different events in one day— a 200-meter run, wrestling, long jump, discus throw, and javelin toss. All events except for wrestling were held in the stadium.

DAY FOUR: The final day of competition started with a 200-meter dash. The rest of the day was devoted to contact sports such as wrestling and boxing. Wrestling contests took place in mud and dust. The dust made it easier to hold onto one's opponent; the mud made it more difficult. To win, an athlete had to pin his opponent's shoulders to the ground three times. This method is still used today. In boxing, athletes wore bronze caps to protect their heads from their opponent's fists. Athletes' fists were covered with hard leather that was studded with metal. The final contact event was a combination of wrestling, boxing, and judo. In this event, athletes could punch, kick, and even strangle their opponents until they surrendered. To complete the Olympic Games, athletes wearing full armor competed in a 400-meter race.

DAY FIVE: The last day was for celebration. This day usually occurred on a full moon and involved more sacrifices to Zeus. The winners' names would be read aloud before the altar of Zeus. These champions would receive a wreath of olive leaves to wear on their heads. Many won prizes such as olive oil, fine horses, and privileges (e.g., not having to pay taxes or being excused from military service). These men returned to their city-states as honored heroes.

Name _____

Chronological Order

PART 1

Directions: Write what happened on the first day of the Greek Olympics.

_____

_____

PART 2

Directions: Tell what happened on the remaining days of the Greek Olympics.

Day	Events
Two	
Three	
Four	
Five	

PART 3

Directions: Number these events in the correct order from 1–5.

_____ 400-meter race

_____ chariot races

_____ pentathlon

_____ wrestling and boxing

_____ celebrations

Chronological Order (cont.)

PART 4

Directions: List the words that the author used to show you the order of events.

_____

_____

PART 5

Directions: Write about your day in chronological order. Be sure to use key words.

_____

_____

_____

_____

Name _____

Comprehension Review

Directions: Fill in the best answer for each question.

1 Which Olympic event happened **first**?

  Ⓐ the pentathlon

  Ⓑ chariot races

  Ⓒ the 200-meter dash

  Ⓓ boxing

2 Which was the **last** event of Day Four?

  Ⓐ the 200-meter run

  Ⓑ boxing

  Ⓒ wrestling

  Ⓓ the 400-meter race

3 Athletes competed **after**

  Ⓐ they celebrated.

  Ⓑ the full moon.

  Ⓒ they trained physically.

  Ⓓ the second day of the Olympics.

4 There were five events in the pentathlon. How many sides do you think are on a <u>pentagram</u>?

  Ⓐ five

  Ⓑ six

  Ⓒ three

  Ⓓ two

5 How was wrestling different from the other events in the pentathlon?

  Ⓐ Athletes did not have to train for wrestling.

  Ⓑ It was not a pentathlon event.

  Ⓒ It was not an Olympic event.

  Ⓓ It was not held in the stadium.

6 What can you guess about Zeus?

  Ⓐ He was an important Greek god.

  Ⓑ He was not important to the Greeks.

  Ⓒ He was a kind of animal.

  Ⓓ He was a Greek slave.

Written Response

Directions: Create a time line showing the events of the Greek Olympics in chronological order. Use short phrases to describe each point on your time line.

Niagara Falls: A Changing Natural Wonder

Niagara Falls is a beautiful part of the Niagara River. This river is part of what separates the United States and Canada. Niagara Falls has two parts: the Horseshoe Falls and the American Falls. Canada owns the U-shaped Horseshoe Falls. The American Falls belongs to the United States. More water goes over Niagara than any other falls in the world. Millions of people visit the Falls each year.

Nature and the Falls

Niagara Falls started out as river rapids. Over time, the rushing water wore away the rock of the riverbed. Different kinds of rock erode at different rates. Hard dolomite covered soft layers of limestone, sandstone, and shale. The rushing water tore away the softer rock. The hard layer was left sticking out like a shelf. Water fell over this shelf. The Falls were born!

Twelve thousand years ago, Niagara Falls was seven miles (11.2 km) downstream. Every year, more rock wore away. This made the Falls move back about three feet (0.9 m) each year. Slowly, the Falls moved upstream. This left behind a deep gorge.

People and the Falls

During the early 1900s, people started diverting water from the river above the Falls. This water flows into a power plant and makes electricity. The water is released back into the Niagara River below the Falls. As the demand for electrical power has increased, more water has been taken. Less water going over the Falls means less erosion. Each year, the American Falls moves back about an inch (2.5 cm). Much more water goes over the Horseshoe Falls. It erodes at least 3 inches (7.6 cm) per year.

Right below the Falls, the water has worn a hole as deep as the Falls is high! When the lower rock layers wear away enough, the upper ledge will fall. This could be dangerous. Scientists keep track of the Falls' edges. They blast away unstable edges so that they won't fall when people are standing on them.

Horseshoe Falls

Name _____

Structure to Predict

PART 1

Directions: In the word web, write details that would help someone make a peanut butter and jelly sandwich.

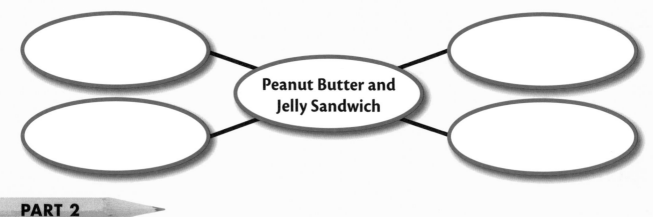

PART 2

Directions: Write the important details you learned about Niagara Falls.

PART 3

Directions: Write what you would learn if each of these headings were added to the passage.

Climate: _____

_____

Wildlife: _____

_____

Vacations: _____

_____

Structure to Predict *(cont.)*

Directions: Write the topic sentence of another text. Then write what you predict the text will tell you about the main idea.

Topic sentence: _____

_____

Prediction: _____

_____

Directions: Read the text and then look back at the prediction you made in Part 4. Tell whether you were right. Then explain how your prediction may have been different from what you read.

_____

_____

_____

_____

Comprehension Review

Directions: Fill in the best answer for each question.

1 This is a _____.

Ⓐ letter

Ⓑ diary

Ⓒ description of a place

Ⓓ biography

4 Which of these is an opinion?

Ⓐ Niagara Falls is a beautiful part of the Niagara River.

Ⓑ Millions of people visit the Falls each year.

Ⓒ During the early 1900s, people started diverting water from the river above the Falls.

Ⓓ Hard dolomite covered soft layers of limestone, sandstone, and shale.

2 *Nature and the Falls*

What will you probably read about in this section?

Ⓐ the number of people who visit Niagara Falls each year

Ⓑ how nature made Niagara Falls

Ⓒ where Niagara Falls is located

Ⓓ how to get to Niagara Falls

5 Which one of these happened **last**?

Ⓐ The Falls erosion decreased.

Ⓑ River rapids caused erosion.

Ⓒ A gorge formed.

Ⓓ The Falls moved upstream.

3 *During the early 1900s, people started diverting water from the river above the Falls.*

What will you read about **next**?

Ⓐ how Niagara Falls was formed

Ⓑ what kinds of wildlife live at Niagara Falls

Ⓒ where Niagara Falls is located

Ⓓ what the diverted water is used for

6 Why has the rate of erosion changed at the Falls?

Ⓐ The Falls have reached a layer of very hard rock.

Ⓑ People have decreased the amount of water that flows over the Falls.

Ⓒ People have built up the edge with cement.

Ⓓ People have blasted away unstable edges.

Name _____

Written Response

Directions: Look at the structure of the passage you read about Niagara Falls. Think about how the headings help you understand what you read. Now come up with new headings of your own that describe the organization of the passage.

MAY THE FORCE BE WITH YOU

Inertia keeps the hockey player gliding across the ice.

A force is anything that pushes or pulls to make an object move. Our world has natural forces. Sir Isaac Newton said that all matter has inertia. Inertia means that any object stays still or moves in the same way until a force acts upon it. For example, a cup placed on a table will stay there until someone or something creates a force to move it. Inertia also means that an ice skate will stay gliding across ice in a straight path until the person wearing it changes direction, falls, or runs out of ice.

Gravity, which pulls everything toward the ground, is a force. Another is magnetic force. Magnets can pull metal objects closer together or push them farther apart.

Friction is an important force, too. Friction works to slow or stop movement between any two surfaces that rub together. Without friction, a person couldn't run. Once that person was moving, he or she couldn't stop. A person couldn't pick up or kick a ball because it would slip away. Hikers wear boots with deep tread to increase friction. Baseball and football players wear cleats for the same reason. A soccer goalie wears gloves to make it easier to catch and hold the ball.

The goalie's gloves apply friction to the ball, and gravity will bring her back down to the ground.

A lack of friction lets things slide. Any smooth surface, such as a kitchen counter, has less friction than a rough surface, such as a brick. Sometimes a lack of friction is good, and other times it's bad. Snow has little friction. This lets skiers glide across it. Cyclists oil the gears on their bikes to make the wheels spin faster. Wet pavement also has little friction. This may cause a car to slide off the road or hit another car.

Drag is a similar force. Drag is the force of air or water slowing down the things that move through them. Engineers design jets and cars to be aerodynamic to reduce drag. Then the object slices through the air, letting it move faster. To cut down on the drag in water, swimmers wear caps. This lets them glide through the water more rapidly. Fish have sleek bodies that can move efficiently through water. People design racing boats to do the same thing.

The swim cap allows the swimmer to glide through the water faster.

Author's Purpose

Directions: Give examples of things that you write and why you write.

What I Write	Why I Write

Directions: Write why you think the author wrote this passage.

_____

_____

Directions: List clues that helped you know that the author wanted to give information.

_____

_____

_____

_____

Author's Purpose (cont.)

Directions: Fill in the chart about author's purpose.

The author wants me to:	The words that the author uses are:

Directions: Write instructions telling someone else how to play a simple game.

_____

_____

_____

_____

Name _____

Comprehension Review

Directions: Fill in the best answer for each question.

1 Why did the author write this passage?

- Ⓐ to explain how forces work
- Ⓑ to get you to buy a racing boat
- Ⓒ to tell a personal story
- Ⓓ to give an opinion about forces

4 Which would want to decrease the force of friction?

- Ⓐ a sledder
- Ⓑ a soccer player
- Ⓒ a mountain climber
- Ⓓ a race car driver

2 *Cyclists oil the gears on their bikes to make the wheels spin faster.*

Why does the author use this example?

- Ⓐ to teach you how to ride a bike safely
- Ⓑ to describe what a bike is
- Ⓒ to get you to buy a bike
- Ⓓ to help explain how friction works

5 Something that is aerodynamic

- Ⓐ flies high.
- Ⓑ cannot crash.
- Ⓒ looks modern.
- Ⓓ glides through air without difficulty.

3 The author hopes that you will

- Ⓐ learn all about Sir Isaac Newton.
- Ⓑ understand how forces work.
- Ⓒ buy a pair of skis.
- Ⓓ learn to play soccer.

6 Which force pulls things toward the ground?

- Ⓐ magnetic
- Ⓑ friction
- Ⓒ gravity
- Ⓓ drag

Name _____

Written Response

Directions: The purpose of this passage is to inform you about forces such as gravity, friction, and drag. Write a paragraph with the purpose of explaining one of the forces. Be sure to state your main idea and include specific details to support it.

Chapter 5: An Eccentric Artist

Diego Rivera

Diego Rivera

One of Diego Rivera's colorful wall murals

Someone tells you to paint a picture. "All right," you think. "No problem. I can fill the canvas pretty easily." But what if the picture you are asked to paint is three stories high, two city blocks long, and one block wide? In other words, a total of 17,000 square feet (1,579 square meters)!

Diego Rivera was one of modern Mexico's most famous painters. When he was asked to paint this huge picture, he did not waver for a minute. In total, Rivera painted 124 frescos, which showed Mexican life, history, and social problems.

A fresco is a painting on wet plaster. Special watercolors are used. Rivera had to plan ahead and sketch what he was going to paint. He used a special plaster. It had to have a certain amount of lime.

Rivera's aides would apply all but the final layer of plaster. Then they used sharp tools to dig the outlines of Rivera's sketches into the plaster. Next, they made a mixture of lime and marble dust. This would be spread over the outline in a thin layer. As soon as this layer was firm—but not dry—Rivera would start to paint.

Every morning, his paints had to be freshly mixed. The pigments had to be ground by hand and mixed on a slab of marble. Rivera would not start working until the paints were perfect. Rivera would paint as long as there was daylight. He could not paint under artificial light. It would change how the colors looked.

Some days, he would say that what he had painted that day was not good enough. Then he would insist that all the plaster be scraped off so he could start again! It took Rivera years to finish, but this mural is thought to be one of the greatest in the world today.

Chapter Titles to Determine Main Ideas

PART 1

Directions: Use the chapter title "An Eccentric Artist" to predict what the passage will be about.

Prediction: _____

_____

_____

PART 2

Directions: Tell whether your prediction from Part 1 was correct. Then add any new information that you learned to update your prediction.

_____

_____

_____

PART 3

Directions: Chapter titles can help you determine the main idea. Write the main idea of the passage.

Main idea: _____

_____

Name _____

Chapter Titles to Determine Main Ideas (cont.)

PART 4

Directions: Use the chapter titles below to answer the questions.

> "Biomes Around the World"   "Life in the Desert"
>
> "The Great Forests"   "Plants and Animals in the Grasslands"

1. What do you predict you will read about in "Life in the Desert"?

   _____

2. Which chapter will likely include general information about biomes?

   _____

3. Where will you read about tropical forests?

   _____

4. What plants or animals might you read about in "Plants and Animals in the Grasslands"?

   _____

PART 5

Directions: Choose a book that has chapters. Then answer the questions below.

1. What is the title of the book?_____

2. What are three of the chapter titles?_____

   _____

   _____

3. Which of the following strategies did you practice: predicting, finding the main idea, or locating

   information? _____

   _____

   _____

Comprehension Review

Directions: Fill in the best answer for each question.

1 You will probably **not** read about _____ in this chapter.

- Ⓐ Diego Rivera's art
- Ⓑ Diego Rivera's early childhood
- Ⓒ where Diego Rivera lived
- Ⓓ the history of Mexico

2 The title tells you that this is **mostly** about

- Ⓐ traveling in Mexico.
- Ⓑ Mexican food.
- Ⓒ how to paint.
- Ⓓ Diego Rivera's art.

3 The title is a clue that this is a

- Ⓐ recipe.
- Ⓑ letter to the editor.
- Ⓒ biography.
- Ⓓ diary.

4 Rivera would start to paint his murals only **after**

- Ⓐ the outline of the painting was dug into the plaster.
- Ⓑ the thin layer of lime and marble dust was firm.
- Ⓒ he chose the perfect location.
- Ⓓ he made a special plaster.

5 *When he was asked to paint this huge picture, he did not waver for a minute.*

What is another word for waver?

- Ⓐ hestitate
- Ⓑ paint
- Ⓒ agree
- Ⓓ run

6 What was the effect of artificial light on paint?

- Ⓐ It made the paint dry more quickly.
- Ⓑ It melted the paint.
- Ⓒ It changed how the colors looked.
- Ⓓ It had no effect on the paint.

Name _____

Written Response

Directions: Imagine that you are the eccentric artist Diego Rivera. Write a letter to a government official explaining why your art is important and how it makes a statement. Include examples to support your response.

Nature's Recycling

Stop! Don't throw dead leaves, grass clippings, and fruit and vegetable peels in the trash. Put them to good use in a compost pile.

Composting is nature's recycling method. It is a simple way to reuse plant waste. Composting breaks down plant materials into soil with lots of minerals. Adding composted soil to a garden helps to grow stronger, healthier plants.

Making your own compost is easy. First, gather "food" for bacteria and fungi. Then, let them do their job. Just follow these easy steps:

1. Choose a spot in your yard to place a bin. You can buy one or make one from wire or wood. It doesn't require a lid. That way, when it rains, the pile will get wet. Water helps the materials decay.

2. Throw kitchen scraps into the pile—things like tea bags, orange rinds, and potato peels. When you cut your grass, add the clippings to the pile. As a general rule, you can add any brown or green plant matter. Although you can put in eggshells, never add animal droppings, cheese, or pieces of meat or fat. These things take a long time to break down.

3. About twice a month, you must turn the pile to allow the rotting materials to get more air. Use a shovel to dig it up a bit. The bacteria and fungi that break down compost need air to live.

After just one year, the compost pile will look like soil. This material is called *humus*. Humus contains many other minerals that plants need. Spread the humus on your garden and watch your plants grow. After they die, add them to the compost pile. Then you can recycle those minerals again!

Name _____

Logical Order

PART 1

Directions: Write three things that need to be written in logical order.

1. _____

2. _____

3. _____

PART 2

Directions: Imagine you are going to tell someone else how to make a compost pile. Write the steps. Make sure you put them in the right order!

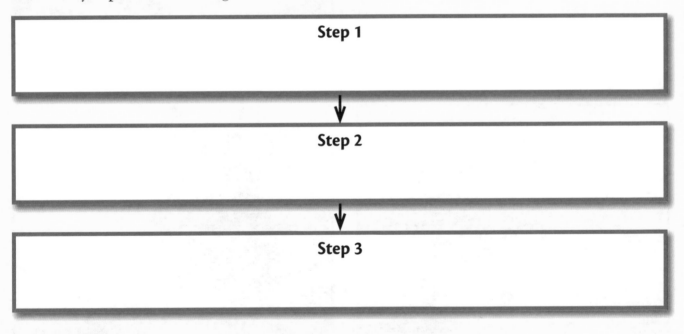

Step 1

↓

Step 2

↓

Step 3

PART 3

Directions: Work with a partner to choose an activity that has to be done in logical order. Write your activity below, along with the steps for the activity.

I want to tell someone how to _____ .

Here are the steps: _____

_____

_____

Name _____

Logical Order *(cont.)*

PART 4

Directions: Use clue words such as *first*, *then*, *after,* and *last* to tell how to make a compost pile.

_____

_____

_____

_____

_____

PART 5

Directions: Write a news report of something that happened in your classroom today. Be sure you put everything in the right order.

_____

_____

_____

_____

_____

Name _____

Comprehension Review

Directions: Fill in the best answer for each question.

1 What should you do **before** throwing scraps into a compost pile?

  Ⓐ Choose a spot in your yard to place a wood or wire bin.

  Ⓑ Turn the pile to allow the rotting materials to get more air.

  Ⓒ Spread the humus on your garden and watch your plants grow.

  Ⓓ Add any brown or green plant matter.

2 What is the **last** step in using compost in your garden?

  Ⓐ Choose a spot in your yard to place a wood or wire bin.

  Ⓑ Turn the pile to allow the rotting materials to get more air.

  Ⓒ Spread the humus on your garden and watch your plants grow

  Ⓓ Gather "food" for bacteria and fungi.

3 Making a compost heap starts with

  Ⓐ adding any brown or green plant matter.

  Ⓑ putting a composting bin in your yard.

  Ⓒ turning the pile to allow the rotting materials to get more air.

  Ⓓ spreading the humus on your garden and watch your plants grow.

4 What is the material in a compost pile called?

  Ⓐ clay

  Ⓑ calcium

  Ⓒ humus

  Ⓓ phosphorous

5 Why does a compost pile need turning?

  Ⓐ so that it won't smell so bad

  Ⓑ so you can reach the humus

  Ⓒ so that it looks better

  Ⓓ so that the rotting material can get more air

6 Which would be good to add to a compost pile?

  Ⓐ pieces of fat cut off a pork chop

  Ⓑ banana peel

  Ⓒ a yogurt cup

  Ⓓ bits of Swiss cheese

Written Response

Directions: Think about how the order of steps in the passage helped you understand composting. Now create your own list of steps to follow for an activity of your choice. Make sure your steps are in logical order.

The Best Baker in the Land

Mrs. Swenson and Mr. Olson each put signs in their bakery windows saying, "The Best Baker in the Land." Back and forth they argued, saying, "I am the best." "No, I am the best." The townspeople soon wearied of their constant bickering.

One day, the mayor announced that the king was coming to look for a new royal baker. "If one of you wins," he told them, "it will be a great honor."

The two bakers baked for days in order to impress the king. When he arrived, he looked over the cakes, cookies, and pies and cried, "But where is the bread?"

The two bakers looked at each other and said, "Bread?"

"You must bake bread for the king!" cried the mayor.

"I have only a little flour and milk left," said Mrs. Swenson.

"I only have a little yeast and butter," said Mr. Olson.

"Fine. Then together you can bake bread," said the king.

Mr. Olson took his yeast and butter over to Mrs. Swenson's bakery. Mrs. Swenson put on her apron, and Mr. Olson put on his hat. The bread was just finished when the mayor ran in yelling, "Hurry! The king is getting impatient." He grabbed the bread from the oven and raced down the street with Mrs. Swenson and Mr. Olson just behind him.

The king tasted the bread and smiled. "This is the best bread I have ever tasted. From now on, you will both be royal bakers and bake my bread together."

Name _____

Fact and Opinion

PART 1

Directions: Write your fact and opinion below.

Fact: _____

Opinion: _____

PART 2

Directions: Read each sentence below. Is it a fact or an opinion? If it is a fact, write an *F* on the line. If it is an opinion, write an *O* on the line.

1. The food in our cafeteria is absolutely disgusting. _____

2. My homework is due tomorrow. _____

3. We watched an excellent movie last night. _____

4. Wearing a helmet while riding a bike helps to keep you safe. _____

5. I am so tired of putting on my school uniform each day. _____

6. The book includes a character named Finn. _____

PART 3

Directions: Look for facts and opinions in the passage. Record them below.

Facts	Opinions
1. _____ _____ 2. _____ _____ 3. _____ _____	1. _____ _____ 2. _____ _____ 3. _____ _____

Name _____

Fact and Opinion (cont.)

PART 4

Directions: Read each sentence below. Change each fact into an opinion.

1. The palm tree on the beach swayed in the wind.

   _____

2. The sunset filled the sky with pink and orange streaks.

   _____

3. My grandmother bakes cookies every Sunday.

   _____

4. The driver of the car slammed on her brakes to avoid the cat in the road.

   _____

5. My bike tire is flat because I ran over a nail.

   _____

PART 5

Directions: Choose another text. Then answer the questions below.

1. What is the title of the text you read?

   _____

2. Is it fiction or nonfiction?

   _____

3. Write one fact from the text.

   _____

4. Write one opinion from the text.

   _____

Comprehension Review

Directions: Fill in the best answer for each question.

1 Which of these is a fact?

ⓐ "The Best Baker in the Land"

ⓑ I am the best.

ⓒ This is the best bread I have ever tasted.

ⓓ The two bakers baked for days to impress the king.

2 Which of these is an opinion?

ⓐ One day, the mayor announced that the king was coming to look for a new royal baker.

ⓑ Mrs. Swenson put on her apron, and Mr. Olson put on his hat.

ⓒ I am the best.

ⓓ Mr. Olson took his yeast and butter over to Mrs. Swenson's bakery.

3 Which one tells what the king thought?

ⓐ This is the best bread I have ever tasted.

ⓑ The two bakers baked for days to impress the king.

ⓒ Mrs. Swenson and Mr. Olson each put signs in the windows of their bakeries.

ⓓ One day, the mayor announced that the king was coming to look for a new royal baker.

4 Which one happened **first**?

ⓐ The king tasted the bread and smiled. "This is the best bread I have ever tasted."

ⓑ Mr. Olson took his yeast and butter over to Mrs. Swenson's bakery.

ⓒ The two bakers baked for days to impress the king.

ⓓ One day, the mayor announced that the king was coming to look for a new royal baker.

5 What problem did Mrs. Swenson and Mr. Olson have?

ⓐ They did not know how to bake bread.

ⓑ They each did not have enough ingredients to bake bread.

ⓒ They did not know the king wanted to choose a new baker.

ⓓ They had no money to buy food.

6 At the **beginning** of the story, Mrs. Swenson and Mr. Olson were _____ of each other.

ⓐ jealous

ⓑ proud

ⓒ glad

ⓓ afraid

Name _____

Written Response

Directions: Imagine that you are the king from the passage you read. Share your opinions about Mrs. Swenson and Mr. Olson's bakeries. Be sure to include facts about them as well as your opinions. If you decide that one baker is better than the other, include details to support your opinion.

OSCAR DE LA HOYA

Oscar De La Hoya was walking five blocks from his home when five men with guns jumped out of a truck. They stole his wallet. When Oscar returned home two hours later, he found his wallet there. The robbers must have realized who he was from his ID card and returned it. Who is Oscar De La Hoya?

Oscar was born on February 4, 1973, in East Los Angeles. He lived in a modest home with his parents, siblings, and grandparents. But there were many problems were he lived: crime, drugs, and gangs. To keep him safe, Oscar's father took him to a boxing gym at the age of six. Oscar was on his way.

In 1992, Oscar flew to Barcelona, Spain. He would compete in the Olympics there. Judging had never been completely fair. It was suspected that some countries were favored over others. But Oscar didn't worry only about beating his opponents—he worried about beating the computer, too.

Oscar De La Hoya's 1992 Olympic boxing victory

To try to make judging more fair, a new computer was set up. But the computer system was just as messy and unfair. Each judge was given a keypad with two buttons. Every time a boxer from the red corner scored, the red keypad was pushed. Every time the boxer from the blue corner scored, the blue keypad was pushed. At least three of the five judges had to press the button within one second for a punch to be recorded. What if the boxer scoring the punches had his back to the judge? What if the punch was thrown with such speed that the judge did not see it? What if the judge was cheating or was not pushing the button on purpose? The computer could not answer these questions.

Despite these concerns, Oscar went on to beat his opponents *and* the computer! He was the only American to win a gold medal in boxing in 1992. After his triumph, Oscar ran around the ring with the flags from the United States and Mexico. He waved the United States flag because he is a U.S. citizen. He waved the Mexican flag to show respect for the country where his parents were born.

Name _____

Meaning Clues to Predict

PART 1

Directions: Write the predictions you made about this passage.

_____

_____

_____

PART 2

Directions: Read your predictions above. Now that you have read the whole passage, think about how accurate your predictions were. Answer the questions below.

1. Did your predictions prove to be true or not true? _____

2. What clues in the text helped you make a prediction?_____

_____

PART 3

Directions: Read the section of text provided by your teacher. Then answer the questions below.

1. What is the title of the text?_____

2. What has happened in the text so far? _____

_____

3. At what point in the text did you stop? Describe it. _____

_____

4. What do you predict will happen next?_____

_____

5. What foreshadowing did the author include in the text? _____

_____

Meaning Clues to Predict *(cont.)*

PART 4

Directions: Reread the answers you wrote in Part 3. Then answer the questions below.

1. Was your prediction correct? _____

2. What information in the text helped you make the prediction? _____

_____

3. Did you change your prediction at any point? _____

4. Why or why not? _____

_____

PART 5

Directions: Answer the questions below.

1. Why is predicting an important skill? _____

_____

2. How can you make smart predictions? _____

_____

3. Why would you predict when you read something in the future? _____

_____

_____

_____

Name _____

Comprehension Review

Directions: Fill in the best answer for each question.

1 What can you predict from the title?

(A) This will be about someone named Oscar De La Hoya.

(B) This will be about how to swim.

(C) This will help you learn to do something.

(D) This will be a letter to the editor.

2 *Oscar De La Hoya was walking five blocks from his home when five men with guns jumped out of a truck.*

What might happen next?

(A) The men gave Oscar money.

(B) The men asked Oscar for directions.

(C) The men stole something from Oscar.

(D) The men got out of the truck.

3 *In 1992, Oscar flew to Barcelona, Spain. He would compete in the Olympics there.*

This sentence helps you predict that you will read about

(A) the climate of Spain.

(B) Oscar De La Hoya's family.

(C) Oscar De La Hoya's childhood.

(D) the Olympic competition.

4 Why did the robbers return Oscar's wallet?

(A) They wanted him to join them.

(B) They realized who he was and didn't want to steal from him.

(C) They didn't find any money in the wallet.

(D) They realized it wasn't really a wallet.

5 *After his triumph, Oscar ran around the ring with the flags from the United States and Mexico.*

What does the word <u>triumph</u> mean?

(A) failure

(B) travel

(C) a great success

(D) a kind of shoe

6 Which word might you use to describe Oscar De La Hoya?

(A) athletic

(B) lazy

(C) shy

(D) unhealthy

Name _____

Written Response

Directions: Write about what makes Oscar De La Hoya's story unique. Think about all that he went through to become the great boxer that he is today. Include examples from the passage to support your response.

UNSEEN VOLCANOES BUILD NEW LAND

No one has ever seen some of the biggest volcanoes. Why not? They lie far below the sea!

The biggest mountain range zigzags all over the ocean floor. Every day, at least one of its volcanoes erupts, causing hot lava to pour out onto the sea floor. The ocean's cold water cools the lava, turning it into rock. Layers of this rock build up. If it reaches above the ocean, it forms an island.

Hawaii and Iceland are volcanic islands. Hawaii is growing. Its active volcanoes still erupt. Their lava adds more land.

The world's newest volcanic island appeared in 1963 near Iceland. Sailors saw a huge cloud of smoke and steam. They sailed closer and saw the birth of a new island. This island kept growing for the next three and a half years.

Even lava that doesn't reach above the sea changes land. Over a long time, the lava on the ocean floor expands and pushes on the continents. This causes them to move a little bit. Each continent moves from one to three inches a year. This means that Earth's surface is always changing. A million years ago, Earth looked different than it does today. A million years from now, it will look different too.

Hot lava flows across land

Cooled lava turns into rock

Purpose for Reading

PART 1

Directions: Answer the questions below.

1. What was the last thing you read? _____

_____

2. What was it about? _____

_____

3. Why did you read it? _____

_____

PART 2

Directions: Write the information that a person could learn from this passage.

_____

_____

_____

PART 3

Directions: Tell whether you would recommend this passage to someone who wanted to learn about volcanoes. Then tell why or why not.

_____

_____

_____

_____

Name _____

Purpose for Reading *(cont.)*

Directions: Answer the first question. Then interview your partner to answer the second question.

1. What is your favorite thing to read? Why?_____

    _____

2. What is your partner's favorite thing to read? Why? _____

    _____

Directions: Think about why someone might read the books below. Write a purpose for each title.

Safety Tips for Skateboarding

Purpose: _____

The Story of the Pioneers

Purpose: _____

Recycle! Don't Waste

Purpose: _____

Easy Chocolate Chip Cookies

Purpose: _____

Comprehension Review

Directions: Fill in the best answer for each question.

1 You would read this if you wanted to

- Ⓐ learn about underwater volcanoes.
- Ⓑ make your own volcano.
- Ⓒ travel to a volcanic island.
- Ⓓ find out what Earth looked like a million years ago.

2 What could this passage help you do?

- Ⓐ plan a vacation to Hawaii
- Ⓑ find a store that sells supplies for making your own volcano
- Ⓒ learn how volcanic islands form
- Ⓓ find out someone's opinion of volcanoes

3 You could **not** use this information to

- Ⓐ find an example of a volcanic island.
- Ⓑ learn how volcanic islands form.
- Ⓒ find out where the world's newest volcanic island is.
- Ⓓ plan a trip to Iceland.

4 Which one happens **last**?

- Ⓐ A volcano erupts under the sea.
- Ⓑ Layers of rock build up, sometimes forming an island.
- Ⓒ Lava pours out onto the sea floor.
- Ⓓ The lava cools, forming rocks.

5 How are Hawaii and Iceland similar?

- Ⓐ They both have tropical climates.
- Ⓑ They are both in the Atlantic Ocean.
- Ⓒ They are both volcanic islands.
- Ⓓ They both belong to the United States.

6 What causes the continents to move a little each year?

- Ⓐ Lava on the ocean floor expands and pushes on them.
- Ⓑ The continents are pulled toward one another by gravity.
- Ⓒ Ocean tides push the continents.
- Ⓓ The continents float on the ocean water.

Name _____

Written Response

Directions: Think about the purpose for reading the passage on volcanoes. Write a summary of the passage. Be sure to include the main idea and important details.

Trouble in the Coral Reefs

Sea turtle

For millions of years, there have been special underwater ecosystems called *coral reefs*. They have provided homes and food for thousands of living things. Fish and sea birds live near the reefs. They share it with giant clams, sea turtles, crabs, starfish, and many others.

Now these beautiful places are in danger. So are all the sea plants and animals near them. Scientists blame it on people and pollution. We have ruined more than one-fourth of Earth's coral reefs. Unless things change, all of the remaining reefs may die soon.

Some people think that coral is stone because it is rough and hard, but coral is an animal! Tiny polyps form coral reefs. They are many different colors. These colors come from the algae living in the coral. The algae are food for the coral polyps.

Red finger sponge

Billions of coral polyps stick together. New ones grow on the skeletons of dead coral. This happens year after year. Over time, the coral builds up a reef. The reef rises from the ocean floor and grows until it almost reaches the sea's surface.

Coral reefs have been harmed in different ways. People have broken off pieces to sell or keep for themselves. To catch more fish, people have dropped sticks of dynamite into the water. This has blown up parts of reefs. Water pollution has caused the sea plants near coral reefs to grow too much. They block the sun that the algae need.

The worst problem is that the world's oceans are heating up. Warm water kills the algae. When the algae die, the coral loses both its food and its color. The coral turns white and dies. Scientists call this process *coral bleaching*. The bleached part of the coral reef cannot recover.

Bleached coral

Name _____

Cause and Effect

Directions: List some things that cause harm to coral reefs.

_____

_____

_____

Directions: Tell how you think pollution from people affects the coral reefs. Then draw a picture to go with your response.

_____

_____

Directions: Think about the effects that people and pollution have on coral reefs. Write what you could tell someone about those effects.

_____

_____

_____

Cause and Effect (cont.)

Directions: Write what would happen if there were no coral reefs. In other words, what would be the effects of having no coral reefs?

_____

_____

_____

_____

Directions: Write the causes and effects that you found in the passage.

Cause	Effect

Name _____

Comprehension Review

Directions: Fill in the best answer for each question.

1 Which one does **not** cause harm to the coral reefs?

- Ⓐ People break off pieces of coral.
- Ⓑ Fish and other wildlife live in the coral reefs.
- Ⓒ People have blown up parts of the reef with dynamite.
- Ⓓ The world's oceans are heating up.

2 What is the effect of the oceans heating up?

- Ⓐ Coral reefs have become much larger.
- Ⓑ Coral reefs attract more fish.
- Ⓒ More coral grows because the water is warmer.
- Ⓓ Warm water kills the algae that feed the coral.

3 What happens when sea plants near the coral reefs grow too much?

- Ⓐ They provide food for more coral reefs.
- Ⓑ They cool the ocean temperature.
- Ⓒ More fish come to feed on them.
- Ⓓ They block the sunlight that algae need.

4 What are coral polyps?

- Ⓐ rocks
- Ⓑ plants
- Ⓒ animals
- Ⓓ algae

5 What is another word for dynamite?

- Ⓐ clay
- Ⓑ explosives
- Ⓒ fire
- Ⓓ poison

6 What will probably happen if all of the coral reefs die?

- Ⓐ Many ocean animals will die.
- Ⓑ The ocean will get colder.
- Ⓒ The ocean will get warmer.
- Ⓓ The ocean will get deeper.

Written Response

Directions: Create a poster that shows the various causes of the harm done to coral reefs. Then write a brief statement telling readers what can be done to help protect the coral reefs.

BLIZZARD!

A blizzard is more than just a bad snowstorm. It's a powerful snowstorm with strong, cold winds. Blizzards usually come after a period of warm winter weather. A mass of cold air moves down from the Arctic Circle and meets the warmer air. The result is a heavy snowfall whipped by bitter north winds. The blowing snow makes it hard to see even a foot or two ahead.

Today, weather reports warn about coming blizzards. But in the past, the dangerous weather came without much warning. A huge blizzard in March 1888 covered the eastern United States, choking New York City. It took more than a week to dig the city out. During that time, many people froze to death.

Blizzards caused trouble for the settlers in the West, too. People had to rush to get themselves and their animals indoors. Otherwise they would have died. Sometimes people were found frozen just a few feet away from their houses or barns. They just couldn't see well enough to find shelter.

It was risky to be out in a storm, yet someone had to feed the animals. So, people tacked one end of a rope to their barns. They nailed the other end of the rope to their houses. They went back and forth holding the rope. This kept them from getting lost in the blinding snow.

Blizzards happen in the U.S. Northern Plains states, in eastern and central Canada, and in parts of Russia. The high winds can blow snow into huge drifts 15 feet (5 m) high. These snowdrifts often stop all travel. Schools and businesses close down for days. All the snow must be cleared away. During that time, snowplows may be the only traffic on the roads.

A huge blizzard covered New York City in 1888.

A snowplow removes snow from a city road.

Name _____

Summary Sentences

PART 1

Directions: Write the first summary sentence from the passage. Then draw a picture to match.

_____

PART 2

Directions: Look for other summary sentences that give important information. Write them here.

_____

_____

PART 3

Directions: Tell what the author wants you to know about blizzards (i.e., the most important things).

_____

_____

_____

_____

Name _____

Summary Sentences (cont.)

PART 4

Directions: Write your own summary sentence for the passage.

_____

_____

PART 5

Directions: Read the newspaper article provided by your teacher. Write a summary sentence that tells what it is about. Then write the main ideas.

Summary sentence: _____

_____

Main ideas: _____

_____

_____

Comprehension Review

Directions: Fill in the best answer for each question.

1 *Blizzards caused trouble for the settlers in the West, too.*

Which detail goes with this sentence?

Ⓐ A huge blizzard in March 1888 covered New York City.

Ⓑ A mass of cold air moves down from the Arctic Circle.

Ⓒ People had to rush to get indoors.

Ⓓ Blizzards happen in North America and Russia.

2 Which sentence tells the most important idea in the passage?

Ⓐ A blizzard is a powerful snowstorm with strong, cold winds and heavy snow.

Ⓑ Blizzards can happen in many different places.

Ⓒ A huge blizzard in March 1888 covered New York City.

Ⓓ Blizzards come from a mass of cold air from the Arctic Circle.

3 Which one is **not** a good summary sentence?

Ⓐ A blizzard is more than just a bad snowstorm.

Ⓑ Blizzards caused trouble for the settlers in the West, too.

Ⓒ But in the past, the dangerous weather came without much warning.

Ⓓ This kept them from getting lost in the blinding snow.

4 How does a blizzard differ from a regular snowstorm?

Ⓐ A blizzard has lots of snow but no wind.

Ⓑ A blizzard has high winds that blow lots of snow around.

Ⓒ A blizzard has high winds but no snow.

Ⓓ No one knows when a blizzard is coming.

5 Why does transportation usually halt during a blizzard?

Ⓐ The snowdrifts bury all vehicles.

Ⓑ Winds blow the vehicles right off the road.

Ⓒ It's too cold for any engine to run.

Ⓓ People can't see well enough to drive or to fly.

6 What does visibility mean?

Ⓐ how well you can smell

Ⓑ how well you can see

Ⓒ how well you can hear

Ⓓ how well you can feel

Name _____

Written Response

Directions: Imagine that you live in a northern plains state where blizzards occur. Pretend that your friend wants to move there. Give your friend a summary of what you know about blizzards to help him or her make a decision about whether to move there.

I WANT TO BE AN EXPLORER

I have always wanted to be an explorer. Columbus, Magellan, Lewis and Clark, and the astronauts are my heroes. I love reading stories about their adventures. It must have been exciting taking off for new places, not knowing what they'd find.

One day in school, we were telling what we wanted to be and do. I said I wanted to be an explorer and find strange and wonderful places. Others laughed and told me there is nowhere left to explore. Even if there was, I am too young to go.

Then my teacher said, "It's not really true that John can't be an explorer or that he is too young. In fact, if he can get someone to take him, he could start exploring strange and interesting places this weekend!"

The class looked puzzled. One of the boys asked, "What would he explore? Where would he go?"

A girl said, "He could explore our garage. My mother says you could get lost in there with all the weird junk." Everyone in the class laughed.

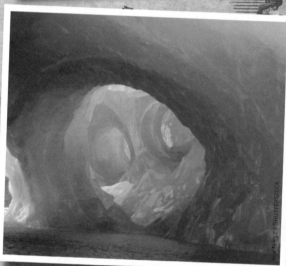

The teacher laughed, too. Then she said, "Exploring your garage might be fun, but there are much better places to go. And they are not that far away."

The teacher took out a paperback book and read the title to the class: *How to Find Unexplored Places Right in Your Own Backyard*. The teacher explained that "in your own backyard" means places close to where you live. She leafed through the book and started reading, "There are ice caves, hot springs, and even an old ghost town near Parkersville."

"That's not far from here!" cried the class.

"Yes. But even if you can't get to Parkersville, you can explore many things right here in our city." She continued reading from the book. It told about the wonders of the big central library. It talked about the nooks and crannies in the old train station. And it even mentioned a few museums we'd never heard of. "So you can be an explorer right where you are, even today," she said. "And you are never too old or too young to start."

The class didn't think it was foolish to want to be an explorer anymore. In fact, quite a few of them decided to become weekend explorers!

Name _____

Retelling

PART 1

Directions: Write four important details from the passage. Tell them in your own words.

1. _____

2. _____

3. _____

4. _____

PART 2

Directions: Write a sentence telling the main idea of the passage. Then draw a picture to match.

Main idea: _____

PART 3

Directions: Fill in the information below.

Main characters: _____

Setting: _____

Plot (what happened): _____

_____

_____

Retelling (cont.)

PART 4

Directions: Fill in the boxes to map out what happens in the passage.

Story Map

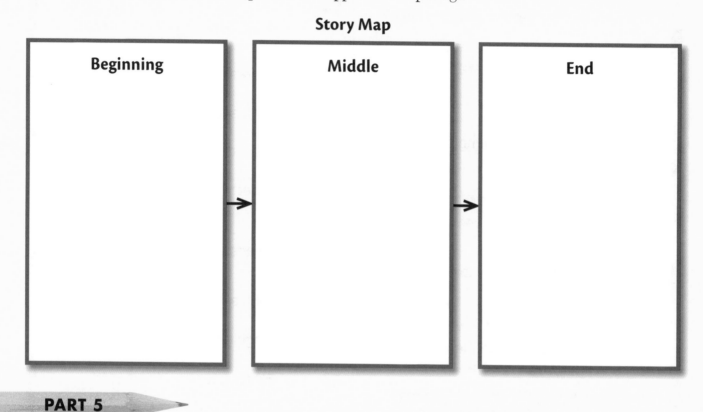

| Beginning | Middle | End |

PART 5

Directions: Use your notes from Parts 1–4. In your own words, tell your partner what this passage is about. Then write the retelling of the passage. Make sure you include the main idea and important details from the passage.

_____

_____

_____

_____

_____

Name _____

Comprehension Review

Directions: Fill in the best answer for each question.

1 How could you tell someone else what <u>in your own backyard</u> means?

- Ⓐ It means someplace close to where a person lives.
- Ⓑ It means in a person's house.
- Ⓒ It means something buried in a garden.
- Ⓓ It means a place that a person owns.

2 Which one explains how the teacher told the class about exploring?

- Ⓐ The teacher asked the students what they wanted to study.
- Ⓑ The teacher told the class that exploring a garage is fun.
- Ⓒ The teacher read to the class about some local places to explore.
- Ⓓ The teacher showed the class some pictures.

3 Which one explains why the class laughed at John's wanting to become an explorer?

- Ⓐ The teacher said he was too young.
- Ⓑ Someone said he didn't have enough experience for that.
- Ⓒ John wanted to be an explorer. The students laughed at his idea.
- Ⓓ Students said that there was nowhere left to explore.

4 *The class looked puzzled.*

In this sentence, the word <u>puzzled</u> means

- Ⓐ interested.
- Ⓑ confused.
- Ⓒ excited.
- Ⓓ upset.

5 From whose point of view is the story told?

- Ⓐ John's best friend
- Ⓑ Magellan
- Ⓒ John
- Ⓓ the teacher

6 What changed the class's point of view about being an explorer?

- Ⓐ John convinced the class that being an explorer is fun.
- Ⓑ The teacher showed them that a person can explore nearby places.
- Ⓒ The teacher admitted that she is an explorer.
- Ⓓ The class went on a field trip.

Name _____

Written Response

Directions: Create a story about a narrator who wants to be an explorer. Tell where he or she goes exploring. Include details about the setting.

ALEXANDER THE GREAT

In 356 B.C., King Philip II and his wife Olympia had a son. They named him Alexander. He was a brave and smart boy who showed strong leadership. One famous tale describes a time when Alexander was only 14 years old. King Philip had brought home a horse to add to his stable. When Philip tried to mount the steed, it bucked and reared. The king was thrown off instantly. He decided that the horse was useless and called for it to be taken away.

Alexander was in the crowd, watching from the sidelines. He insisted that the great horse was being wasted. Many people thought that Alexander's remarks were bold because he was only a young boy. But the king challenged Alexander to tame the horse. He promised him that he could keep it if he was successful.

According to legend, the horse instantly calmed when Alexander got close to him. He patted the stallion's neck and spoke softly in his ear. The horse let Alexander lead him. Alexander had noticed that the horse did not like the sight of his great shadow on the ground. Gently, he turned the horse away from its shadow and was able to swing into the saddle without any trouble.

Alexander rode away and back to his father. The crowd cheered this victory and his father wept in joy. The king gave his son the horse, saying, "My boy, you must find a kingdom big enough for your ambitions. Macedonia is too small for you."

The horse was proud and loyal, allowing no one but Alexander to ride him as long as he lived. According to legend, the horse would even lower his body to let Alexander mount him more easily. For years, Alexander rode the valiant horse and friend into many battles.

This legend describes some of Alexander's special qualities that allowed him to conquer lands and still maintain respect as a great leader. He earned the name Alexander the Great.

A statue of Alexander the Great

Name _____

Topic to Predict

PART 1

Directions: Think about what this story will be about. Write your prediction.

_____

_____

PART 2

Directions: Think about what will happen in the rest of the passage. Write your prediction and draw a picture of it.

_____

PART 3

Directions: If this were a book, predict what the next chapter might be about. Write your prediction below.

_____

_____

Topic to Predict (cont.)

PART 4

Directions: Write what you think happened to Alexander.

_____

_____

_____

PART 5

Directions: Fill in the information below.

1. This book's title is _____ .

2. It will probably be about _____

_____ .

Name _____

Comprehension Review

Directions: Fill in the best answer for each question.

1 This passage is about Alexander the Great. You will probably learn

   Ⓐ where and when Alexander lived.

   Ⓑ how to make Greek food.

   Ⓒ where Greece is located.

   Ⓓ about a new sport.

2 Which piece of information will probably **not** be in this passage?

   Ⓐ where Alexander lived

   Ⓑ something that happened to Alexander

   Ⓒ how the Greeks built their houses

   Ⓓ when Alexander was born

3 Because this is the story of Alexander the Great, it is probably a

   Ⓐ set of instructions.

   Ⓑ recipe.

   Ⓒ letter to the editor.

   Ⓓ biography.

4 What caused King Philip to decide his horse was useless?

   Ⓐ The horse would not move.

   Ⓑ The horse threw him off.

   Ⓒ The horse was too small.

   Ⓓ The horse bit him.

5 *When Philip tried to mount the steed, it bucked and reared.*

What does <u>bucked and reared</u> tell you about the horse?

   Ⓐ It was energetic.

   Ⓑ It was asleep.

   Ⓒ It was hungry.

   Ⓓ It was calm.

6 Alexander was probably

   Ⓐ lazy.

   Ⓑ shy.

   Ⓒ very weak.

   Ⓓ brave.

Name _____

Written Response

Directions: Think about how Alexander the Great is described in the passage. Tell what kind of person you think he was. Include examples from the passage to support your response.

ANCIENT GREECE

Greece is located on the southern tip of Europe. It borders the Aegean, Adriatic, and Mediterranean seas. Greece has a large mainland surrounded by many smaller islands. It is a hot, dry country with mountain ranges.

RELIGION

Ancient Greek life centered on religion. Greeks worshipped many gods and goddesses. The Greeks thought that the gods controlled every part of people's lives. Big decisions about war and marriage were made only after checking with the gods. Even small decisions were made this way. Poseidon was the god of the seas and rivers. Apollo controlled the sun and light. Aphrodite was the goddess of love and beauty. Athena was the goddess of war and wisdom.

ART AND THEATER

The ancient Greeks made statues and beautiful temples for the gods. Huge wall paintings decorated these buildings. They were called *murals*. The ruins of these buildings remain, but the paint wore away long ago. Early Greek plays had religious themes. Later plays began to deal with politics. In 534 B.C., the first public plays were held in Athens. They were performed in open-air theaters shaped like semicircles. Seats were built into the hillsides. Some ancient Greek plays are still performed.

SCIENCE AND MEDICINE

The ancient Greeks were interested in science. They made advances in biology, mathematics, astronomy, and geography. They based what they knew on what they observed in the world. They were the first people in Europe to do this.

An important area of science for the Greeks was medicine. Long ago, the Greeks thought that illness was a punishment from the gods. Sanctuaries were built all over Greece. These were holy places to honor the god of medicine. People would spend the night at a sanctuary and pray for a cure. Later, the Greeks came up with treatments for diseases. A Greek doctor named Hippocrates came up with many of these treatments. He is called the Father of Modern Medicine.

Name _____

Typeface

Directions: Look at the passage. Notice the appearance of the text on this page. Write your observations below.

_____

_____

_____

Directions: You are learning about typeface. Explain how different kinds of typeface can be useful to a reader.

_____

_____

_____

Directions: One example of typeface on the page you read is the title. The title gives the reader a clue about the main idea of the passage. Write what you think the main idea of the passage is.

_____

_____

_____

Typeface (cont.)

PART 4

Directions: Choose a text that has different typefaces. Then answer the questions below.

1. Why did you choose your text example?

   _____

2. How did the typeface on the page help you locate information?

   _____

3. What does the typeface tell you about the main idea of the text?

   _____

PART 5

Directions: Fill in the information below.

Typeface example #1: _____

Typeface example #2: _____

What the text says: _____

Did this typeface help you determine the main idea? _____

The main idea is: _____

_____

Did this typeface help you locate information? _____

How? _____

_____

Name _____

Comprehension Review

Directions: Fill in the best answer for each question.

1 The typeface tells you that _____ is an important topic in this passage.

Ⓐ life in a Greek home

Ⓑ Greek food

Ⓒ Greek theater and art

Ⓓ Greek rivers

2 Which one is **not** an important topic in this passage?

Ⓐ Greek religion

Ⓑ the first public plays

Ⓒ Greek science

Ⓓ Greek art

3 Why is *Religion* in large typeface?

Ⓐ It is the first topic.

Ⓑ It is not very important.

Ⓒ It comes before a paragraph.

Ⓓ It is an important topic.

4 You would probably **not** see _____ if you visited Greece.

Ⓐ an icecap

Ⓑ the Adriatic Sea

Ⓒ a mountain

Ⓓ an island

5 Why did the Greeks check with the gods before making most decisions?

Ⓐ Greek law said that they had to check with the gods.

Ⓑ They did not have enough information to make decisions.

Ⓒ They thought the gods controlled every part of people's lives.

Ⓓ Most Greeks did not believe the gods were important.

6 If the Greeks wanted to win a big battle, they would probably check with _____ before fighting.

Ⓐ Poseidon

Ⓑ Athena

Ⓒ Apollo

Ⓓ Hippocrates

Name _____

Written Response

Directions: Describe what you notice about the typeface used in this passage. Then tell what purpose it serves for the reader.

School Garbage

There is too much garbage at our school. Have you ever noticed how full the trash cans are at the end of the day? If you looked through the trash cans, you would find plastic, foam, glass bottles, food waste, paper, and much more. Many of these items can be recycled, or we could avoid their use altogether.

One solution to the problem is to set up a recycling program at our school. Next to the trash cans, we could have recycling bins for paper, cans, and plastic. In every classroom, there could be a recycling bin for paper. Students could be in charge of running the recycling program once it is in place.

Another solution is for students and teachers to think about how they pack their lunches. Instead of paper lunch bags, we could bring reusable cloth bags or tin lunch boxes. We could use reusable plastic containers instead of plastic bags. We could bring cloth napkins instead of paper ones. We could also bring real silverware instead of plastic. And how about all the juice boxes and soda cans we bring? Instead, we could use a reusable sports bottle for our drinks.

If both of these ideas were put in place, we would have a lot less garbage at our school.

Proposition and Support

PART 1

Directions: Write what the problem is. Draw a picture to match.

Problem: _____

PART 2

Directions: Write the two proposed solutions to the problem.

1. _____

2. _____

PART 3

Directions: Write the key words from the passage that tell you that it is a proposition-and-support text.

Key words: _____

_____

Name _____

Proposition and Support *(cont.)*

PART 4

Directions: With a partner, propose another solution to the problem.

_____

_____

PART 5

Directions: Write a problem and one solution to the problem. Then write information to support your proposed solution.

Problem: _____

_____

Solution: _____

_____

Support: _____

_____

_____

_____

Comprehension Review

Directions: Fill in the best answer for each question.

1 *There is too much garbage at our school.*

Which sentence supports this?

- (A) Bring a reusable cloth bag or a tin lunch box.
- (B) We could also bring real silverware.
- (C) Many of these items can be recycled.
- (D) Have you ever noticed how full the trash cans are?

2 Which of these is a solution to the problem of too much garbage?

- (A) The trash cans are too full.
- (B) And how about all the juice boxes and soda cans we bring?
- (C) There is too much garbage at our school.
- (D) Next to the trash cans, we could have recycling bins.

3 *And how about all the juice boxes and soda cans we bring?*

Which sentence is a solution to this problem?
- (A) In every classroom, there could be a recycling bin for paper.
- (B) Bring a reusable cloth bag or a tin lunch box.
- (C) Instead, we could use reusable sports bottles for our drinks.
- (D) We could bring cloth napkins instead of paper ones.

4 *Students could be in charge of running the recycling program once it is in place.*

In this sentence, what does <u>once it is in place</u> mean?

- (A) after the program has been set up
- (B) after the program sat down
- (C) after the program stopped
- (D) after the program has a location

5 The author would probably agree that

- (A) fast-food bags are a good idea.
- (B) people should bring more soda cans to school.
- (C) it doesn't matter how much you throw away.
- (D) everyone can help reduce the amount of garbage at school.

6 What is the author's purpose?

- (A) to get you to buy something
- (B) to persuade you to do something
- (C) to inform you about something
- (D) to share a personal experience

Name _____

Written Response

Directions: Write a letter to a school administrator. Tell about the garbage problem at your school. Give at least one idea for how to solve this problem.

Johnson Space Center

The United States is one of the leading countries for training astronauts. Astronauts in the United States begin their training at the Johnson Space Center in Houston, Texas. The center was first opened in 1961.

The Johnson Space Center has a famous room called the Mission Control Center. This is where people on Earth direct the space missions and talk to astronauts in space. They help the astronauts with the work they are doing. The Mission Control Center also watches over the astronauts and their spacecrafts to be sure they are safe.

The Johnson Space Center was named in honor of former president Lyndon B. Johnson, a Texas native. He was president in the 1960s during a worldwide push to land people on the moon for the first time.

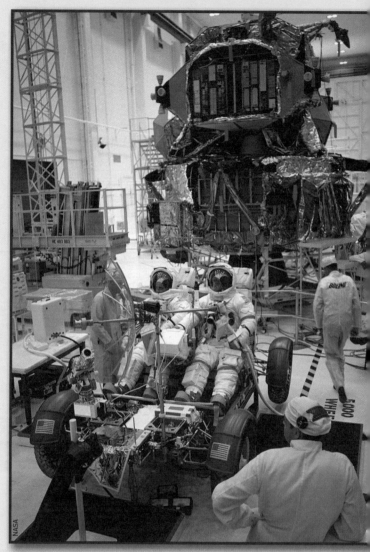

Astronauts in training

Mission Control Center

What do astronauts do at the Johnson Space Center? They spend a lot of time in class, just as you do in school. They must learn the many skills they will need during their space travels.

Astronauts travel into space in groups. So, they train with people they will work with in space. It is very important that astronauts work together as a team. Every person has a job to do. They succeed or fail together, just as any team does.

Astronauts also have to work with people on Earth who help them during their trips into space. These people work in the Mission Control Center. There is a lot of teamwork needed in space travel!

Name _____

Summarizing

Directions: Choose 10 important words from the passage and write them below.

_____

_____

_____

Directions: Fill in the graphic organizer below with the main idea of the passage and key ideas from the paragraphs.

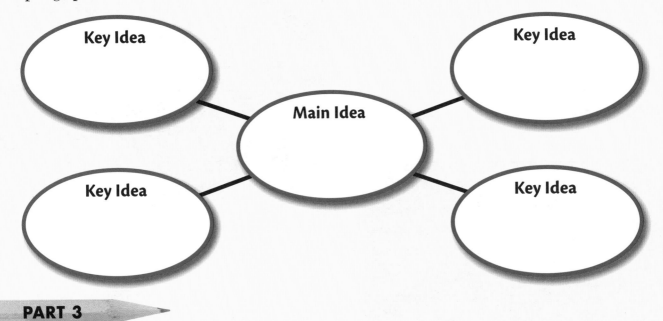

Directions: Read the passage carefully. Follow your teacher's directions to complete the outline.

A. _____

   1. _____

   2. _____

   3. _____

   4. _____

Summarizing (cont.)

PART 4

Directions: Read the passage carefully. Then write a one-paragraph summary of it. You may use your notes and graphic organizers from this lesson's activities about summarizing.

_____

_____

_____

_____

_____

PART 5

Directions: Read the passage carefully. Then reread your summary in Part 4. Next read through the following checklist and determine whether you can answer "yes" to all of the questions. If not, edit your summary as needed.

1. Does the summary tell all the important ideas? _____

2. Does the summary tell the information accurately? _____

3. Does the summary leave out the little details? _____

4. Would someone reading this summary learn what is needed to understand the topic?

   _____

5. Are the ideas in the right order to make sense? _____

6. Are my opinions left out? _____

Name _____

Comprehension Review

Directions: Fill in the best answer for each question.

1 Which one of these **best** summarizes the second paragraph?

- Ⓐ What do astronauts do at the Johnson Space Center?
- Ⓑ The Johnson Space Center has a famous Mission Control Center.
- Ⓒ The Mission Control Center has people who talk to astronauts and help them with their work.
- Ⓓ Astronauts work with the team at the Mission Control Center.

2 Which one is a good summary of what astronauts do at the Johnson Space Center?

- Ⓐ They go to class, train with a team, and work with the people at the Mission Control Center.
- Ⓑ They go to class.
- Ⓒ They train with the people they will work with in space.
- Ⓓ They work with the Mission Control Center team.

3 How could you tell someone how the Johnson Space Center got its name?

- Ⓐ It is named for President Johnson, who was from Texas.
- Ⓑ It is named for President Lyndon Johnson, who was president during the 1960s when there was a push to land people on the moon.
- Ⓒ It got its name from a president who wanted to go to the moon.
- Ⓓ It is in Houston, Texas.

4 Why do you think the Johnson Space Center is located in Texas?

- Ⓐ Other states did not want to have a space center.
- Ⓑ The climate of Texas is best for space travel.
- Ⓒ There was a worldwide push during the 1960s to land a person on the moon.
- Ⓓ President Lyndon B. Johnson was from Texas.

5 What is the purpose of this passage?

- Ⓐ to inform
- Ⓑ to give an opinion
- Ⓒ to persuade
- Ⓓ to tell a personal story

6 Which one is **not** something that astronauts do at the Johnson Space Center?

- Ⓐ go to class
- Ⓑ train with a team
- Ⓒ watch over astronauts and spacecraft
- Ⓓ work with the team at the Mission Control Center

Written Response

Directions: Imagine that you work at the Johnson Space Center and you've just gone on a trip into space with a crew of astronauts. Write a summary of your experience there. Be sure to include the most important details.

An Energetic World

OLLY / SHUTTERSTOCK

Do you know what makes the clouds move across the sky? Do you know how they formed there in the first place? Something makes the trees grow taller. The birds use something all day long to help them fly, feed, and stay safe from predators. That something is energy. Even the car you drove to the park needed energy to get there.

Energy from the Sun

Believe it or not, almost all the energy used at the park came from the sun. The sun is a giant ball of hot gases with a lot of energy. That energy is sent to Earth through heat and light radiation. The sun creates so much energy that it is always shooting out photons. Photons are tiny packets of energy. They travel quickly through space until they arrive at Earth.

Some photons hit air molecules in the atmosphere. Then those air molecules become warmer. The air on the side of the planet facing the sun heats up more than the side facing away. Hot air expands and cold air restricts. So, the hot air spreads out to where the cold air is shrinking. When this happens, winds are created.

Photons also hit water molecules in the oceans and other water bodies. These molecules become warmer, too. Some of them heat so much that they become gaseous and evaporate. Because they are warm, they rise into the atmosphere. Soon after, they arrive at the top where the air is colder. There they condense into water vapor and become clouds.

Other photons hit chlorophyll molecules stored in tree leaves. Those molecules grab the energy in the photons. They use the energy to nourish the tree by making food. The tree uses that food to grow and produce new seeds and fruit. Some of the photons hit the birds, but the birds don't use those photons much. Instead, they eat the energy-filled seeds and fruit from the trees and other plants, which were energized by the photons. The birds use the energy from their food to fly, grow, and reproduce.

When dinosaurs lived, the plants used photons from the sun to store energy. When the plants died and got buried underground, the energy remained in the plants. These plants were squeezed and compressed over millions of years. In time, the plants turned into oil. The oil was then converted into gasoline and pumped into your car.

Questioning

PART 1

Directions: Fill in the first column of the chart below.

Questions I Have Before Reading	Questions I Have While Reading	Questions I Have After Reading

PART 2

Directions: Finish filling in the chart above.

PART 3

Directions: Think of two questions you have about the text. Large thought-provoking questions help you analyze text. Small clarifying questions help you understand text. Write one of each type of question below.

Large question: _____

_____

Small question: _____

_____

Name _____

Questioning *(cont.)*

PART 4

Directions: Fill in the chart below.

Questions I Have Before Reading	Questions I Have While Reading	Questions I Have After Reading

PART 5

Directions: Decide whether these questions are large or small. Write an *L* for large or an *S* for small.

1. Why was there tension between settlers and American Indians? _____

2. What is your Adam's apple? _____

3. What year was the Bill of Rights written? _____

4. Why was slavery accepted by people in colonial America? _____

5. How can all people help keep Earth clean? _____

6. Who was the governor of New York in 1960? _____

7. What is the connection between fast food and obesity? _____

8. What is an amphibian? _____

Name _____

Comprehension Review

Directions: Fill in the best answer for each question.

1 *What is a photon?*

Which sentence answers this question?

Ⓐ The sun is a giant ball of hot gases with a lot of energy.

Ⓑ Some of them heat so much that they become gaseous and evaporate.

Ⓒ Photons are tiny packets of energy.

Ⓓ Photons travel quickly through space.

2 Which question is **not** answered in this passage?

Ⓐ How are winds created?

Ⓑ What do birds do with the energy from the food they eat?

Ⓒ How do photons get to Earth?

Ⓓ How did dinosaurs use energy?

3 *The photons travel quickly through space until they arrive at Earth.*

Which question does this answer?

Ⓐ How big are photons?

Ⓑ How does the sun's energy get to Earth?

Ⓒ How does the sun get energy?

Ⓓ How do clouds move?

4 Unlike hot air, cold air _____.

Ⓐ restricts

Ⓑ helps to form winds

Ⓒ is made of air molecules

Ⓓ can be found on Earth

5 The **main** purpose of the passage is to

Ⓐ get you to use less gas.

Ⓑ explain how photons travel through space.

Ⓒ convince you to help save the planet.

Ⓓ show how all things are connected through energy.

6 Why do trees need chlorophyll?

Ⓐ Chlorophyll turns plants into oil.

Ⓑ Chlorophyll attracts birds, which eat trees' seeds.

Ⓒ Chlorophyll captures energy and produces food.

Ⓓ Chlorophyll creates leaves.

Name _____

Written Response

Directions: Imagine that you work for an environmental company looking for alternative energy sources. You are interviewing a well-known scientist to gather more information for your company. Compile a list of at least 8–10 questions on energy for the scientist you are interviewing.

Glossary

active—erupting often (volcanoes)

adventures—exciting trips or journeys

aerodynamic—made to move easily through air

agreement—a situation in which everyone agrees about an idea

agriculture—the practice of growing crops for people to eat

algae—simple plants that live in or near water

ambitions—goals that a person wants to achieve

ambitious—wanting to be successful

annual—happening once a year

astronauts—people who travel into space

astronomy—the study of stars, planets, and space

bacteria—small living things that feed on other living things or formerly living things

basement—a room below the ground

bickering—arguing

blizzard—a bad snowstorm with strong, cold winds

bound—to be tied up

cells—the smallest units of living matter than can function on their own

chlorophyll—the green pigment, or color, found in the chloroplasts of plants

climates—the types of weather that places have (e.g., hot, dry, humid)

competitions—organized events in which athletes or teams compete against each other

compost—a pile of leaves, grass, fruits, and other scraps recycled naturally into the earth

conquer—to win control over someone or something

constant—without stopping

Glossary (cont.)

crate—a wooden box used for carrying things

crust—the outside layer of Earth's surface

decay—to naturally break down

decisions—choices made

declared—stated what will happen

destination—a place that someone is traveling to

destroy—to put out of existence; to kill

dictator—a leader with absolute power

disappointment—a feeling of sadness because something is not what you expected

eccentric—behaving in a way that is different from most people

ecosystems—communities of organisms and their environments

elected—chosen for a position

energy—power that is produced

erode—to slowly wear away

erupt—to push out smoke, rock, and lava (volcanoes)

exhale—to breathe out

expands—becomes larger

explorer—someone who travels to unknown places to find out about them

fault—a crack in the land caused by crust movement

former—having a certain position in the past, but not now

fossils—parts of animals or plants that lived long ago, usually found in rock

frescos—types of paintings done on lime-plaster with water-based paints

fungus—a living thing like a plant, but without leaves, that grows where it is wet

Glossary (cont.)

general—a high-ranking officer in the military

gnawed—chewed

gorge—a narrow valley between two hills or mountains

gravity—the pulling force that keeps things on the ground

inertia—property of matter that means objects remain moving or at rest until a force acts upon them

inhale—to breathe in

inherited—received as a gift after someone dies

mass—a large amount of something

mercy—willingness to forgive and show kindness

microscope—an instrument used by scientists that enables them to see tiny things

minerals—natural substances that your body needs in order to stay strong and healthy

modest—not very big or fancy

molecules—the smallest parts of substances that cannot be divided without changing form

mural—a large painting done on a wall

muscles—parts of the body that move bones and make organs work

object—a goal; an idea

opponent—someone you compete against

organs—parts of your body with specific purposes

photons—basic units of electromagnetic radiation, or energy

piers—walkways over large bodies of water

plantation—a large farm

politics—the art or science concerned with how the government is run

Glossary *(cont.)*

pollution—things that make the air, water, or soil unclean

program—a plan or idea that is put in place in order to reach a goal

puzzled—confused

recycling—the process of breaking down glass, plastic, paper, etc. so it can be used again

reptiles—cold-blooded animals that move on small, short legs (such as lizards, crocodiles, and dinosaurs)

respect—to have a good opinion of someone

reusable—able to be used again

sanctuaries—sacred or holy places

sand dunes—hills and ridges of sand formed by strong winds

scooted—moved swiftly

siblings—brothers and sisters

sportsmanship—the act of showing fairness and respect whether you win or lose

stationery—things such as envelopes and paper you use for writing

struggled—had difficulty with

substance—any solid or liquid

tinny—thin in tone (as in music, voices, or other sounds)

train—to prepare by practicing

triumph—a win or a great success

tutors—people who teach others, usually individually

unstable—not safe or reliable

warning—a sign or signal that something bad is going to happen

wearied—to become tired